CW00554616

A Letter to My Children from the Fifties

BY THOMAS DAVIDSON

DORRANCE
PUBLISHING CO
EST. 1920
PITTSBURGH, PENNSYLVANIA 15238

The contents of this work, including, but not limited to, the accuracy of events, people, and places depicted; opinions expressed; permission to use previously published materials included; and any advice given or actions advocated are solely the responsibility of the author, who assumes all liability for said work and indemnifies the publisher against any claims stemming from publication of the work.

All Rights Reserved
Copyright © 2022 by Thomas Davidson

No part of this book may be reproduced or transmitted, downloaded, distributed, reverse engineered, or stored in or introduced into any information storage and retrieval system, in any form or by any means, including photocopying and recording, whether electronic or mechanical, now known or hereinafter invented without permission in writing from the publisher.

Dorrance Publishing Co
585 Alpha Drive
Pittsburgh, PA 15238
Visit our website at *www.dorrancebookstore.com*

ISBN: 979-8-8860-4051-7
eISBN: 979-8-8860-4952-7

A Letter to My Children
from the Fifties

Preface

The Fifties: I hear many young people of today complain how bad they have it compared to their parents and grandparents. Especially the grandparents, "The Baby Boomers," who this younger generation claims had a silver spoon in their mouths while growing up!

Really? The *real* fifties was the era of: baloney skin tires, knee patched jeans, darning holes in socks, kids' mouths washed out with soap, hand me down clothes, working after school, collecting empty soda bottles for spending money and more.

So, you want to know the truth and hardships of the fifties, read on!

This book began as a document I started for my children and grandchildren to help ground them in this overly capitalistic society in which we live.

In today's world everyone seems to want everything for themselves and the hell with everyone else. This seems especially relevant in our country's youngest generations as they want everything for nothing, including, but not limited to, education, food, housing and transportation; you name it and they want it for free.

Unfortunately for our nation, most people view the past through the eyes of the present, such as, racism. Racism is and always was a tragedy and scourge on the American image, both at home and across the world. As seen through the eyes of all races from the perspective of today's world, many younger people think that in olden days the entire white population was either middle or upper class. That could not be farther from the truth, as up until the early fifties, about ninety percent of the U.S population lived under the poverty line, both black and white. As blacks moved north during the thirties, they did so to find better jobs as all the U.S. industry was located in the North and the South had yet to recover nearly sixty years after the Civil War had ended. To recover from the carnage left by Civil War, General William Tecumseh Sherman's famous, for the North, infamous for the South, "March to the Sea." Sherman's march was not just a march but a plan devised by him and General Ulysses S. Grant to devastate the South and force them to surrender. In their plan, Sherman and his troops were instructed to burn everything in their path to the ground. That is, every factory, farm, store and town in their path was burned, providing an ever-lasting and devastating effect on both the white and black Southern populations that left no jobs or means to feed their families. Thus, the ever-lasting poverty eventually forced the black population to move north during the thirties clashing with their poor white counter parts already living in the North. The poor whites, like the blacks, were desperate for jobs to feed their starving families due to the Great Depression. This had a devastating effect on the northern white population that had been sympathetic to the blacks' plight during the Civil War, as now they saw the blacks competing for jobs. Unfortunately, the northern migration clashed bitterly between the races and also led to a perception in the North that whites were better than blacks. The desperate whites would do anything to secure jobs and used the perception that whites were better as tool to secure jobs. Unfortunately, that perception was used over and over again, well into the sixties and blacks were typically only hired for manual or labor jobs.

To sum up my feelings above, it was really two uneducated and desperate segments of our population who unfortunately clashed trying to save their families that led greatly to some of the racism that followed in subsequent years and decades. Therefore, in my opinion, it is not fair to look at those events from today's perspective and criticize those past generations as those were desperate times and desperate people of their era and could not envision the ever-lasting effect it has had on our nation.

In today's world, many Americans also believe slavery began in the U.S. However, slavery was ingrained in all the ancient governments and was the engine that built all the great nations of the world since the beginning of time. You don't have to believe me, just look it up in a history book. Romans and Egyptian engineers designed the Great Pyramids, Roman Coliseum and other wonders of the world. But the citizens of Egypt and Rome did not build their kingdoms, slaves did. Attila the Hun conquered all of Asian by destroying villages and taking slaves to do the dirty work. Still other slaves were forced to fight in his armies. African, North American and South American Indian tribes fought and conquered each other for thousands of years and the winners always took slaves. Although black slavery in the South is greatly publicized, indentured slavery was also widely used throughout the southern states during the Colonial Period and up to just prior to the Civil War Era. As wealthy English Londoners were anguish to make their mark on the New World and increase their wealth, they and friends higher up in the English government devised a plan to do just that. The plan was two-fold. Step one was an agreement by the government to free their worst prisoners from overly crowded jails. Secondly, in the agreement, was to have those prisoners sign another agreement with slave traders and Southern plantation owners to be shipped to South Carolina as indentured slaves. The signed agreement stipulated that the indentured slaves would serve a stipulated amount of slave years depending on how severe their crimes had been back in England. When that slavery term was completed, they would become free men. However, many of them tried to escape, the same as black slaves had before them. Like the black slaves, when caught, the white slaves were whipped or in the case of repeat offenders, hung, in public squares as a warning to others. This is mostly how the state of South Carolina was founded, as a slave state.

Most people today do not know that immigration was also a serious problem beginning in the late 1800s until the 1920s and '30s. The problem at that time was not Hispanics but Europeans. As America was initially colonized mostly by the English, it remained mostly populated by Englishmen for a century to come. Then around the mid-1850s, the Irish famine struck Ireland and people were starving. To improve their lot in life, they began moving their families to America. Thus started the first great European migration to America. As the British had fought with and hated the Irish for centuries, the Irish were treated like dirt. Arriving in America, they were met with scorn and only allowed to get jobs that no one else would do, such as shoveling manure, scraping off and disposing of bed pan excrements in cobble stone streets and the like. Then in the late 1800s the Italians began to arrive as dire poverty and hardship drove thousands upon thousands to our nation each year for the next decade. Again, they were greeted by scorn, as the Italians arriving on our shores spoke no English whatsoever. Next, the Polish arrived, followed closely by other European nationalities. Each new nationality arriving was treated as badly as the first, as none of them could speak English. Thus, the term "American Melting Pot" was born. The only difference between then and now was the government totally controlled the flow of immigration back then. Only those properly processed were allowed in legally. Whereas today the government makes no attempt whatsoever to control the flow and no one truly knows if they are properly processed.

To help address these issues, it is time for the media and politicians to lighten up on the race and immigrations issues until the government takes action on both issues. Is there still racism, absolutely! But each of us should take the time to read our history, not just take the word of professors, politicians and the news media, who hope to gain financially or politically from putting their own spin on it. It is worth the effort of all Americans to independently learn how far we have come in eradicating racism from our society and not take the word of others. This can only be done by reading history books and listening learning from our past as told by older relatives or friends who lived through those eras. After all, we are all Americans, just thriving through the day and trying to make a better life for ourselves and families. Our great nation was built not from individual black, white, Asian or Indian cultures, but collectively as, if again you read your history, we are the melting pot of the world. By bringing all cultures together as one gives our nation great strength, that no other can ever conquer as long as we remain as one! Also, no one, and I mean no one enjoys food as much as Americans! No other country in the world enjoys as many diversified foods as the U.S. Who doesn't enjoy Chinese, Italian, Latin, Asian, French, Greek, or African cuisines? There also are various other fantastic dishes derived internally from mixing cultures such as Soul food, Southern dishes derived from African roots and then there is the Tex-Mex delicacies enjoyed in the in the Southwest region of our country. Tired of chowing down on those favorites, try Moroccan, Vietnamese or Turkish meals for the palate to enjoy! Additionally, take time to enjoy community festivals to get a flavor of other countries' cultures without ever leaving the states!

It is well past time for all venues to stop telling Americans how bad our country has become. Let us collectively enjoy all it has to offer from melting all those worldly cultures into one great one, which is of course, the U.S.A.

I wrote this book not for fortune, fame or notoriety but to reflect upon not only my love for our country but also past generations when the average guy only got what they earned and were thus rewarded accordingly. As I am writing this book to my children and grandchildren, I am writing from my own and at times, their perspective in referring to family members throughout the book. My thoughts are my own and not of family members or others.

This book is dedicated to my present and past family members and other hardy souls who came before us, thus paving a way forward for our great nation to succeed. Hopefully, this book will in some way redirect our country's ship's direction, in a better and more moral direction, as I now see the earth as flat as in the earliest generations and our ship about to fall into the abyss unless we change direction.

Chapter 1

I grew up in the 1950s in a small two-bedroom home that had no basement and was located within the community known as Overlea, MD. The community was situated only a few blocks outside Baltimore City limits. As was common in those days, most city neighborhood communities were rough and you had to be tough, or at least act tough growing up, as there were occasional territorial fights among teenagers who would encroach on other kids' territories. My older brother, Frankie, was a great brother to have growing up in a tough neighborhood and he loved me dearly. I know how much he loved me because, to toughen me up, he would hit me on the arms until I had bruises, kick me in the butt and push me to the floor, whenever he could get away with it. When these various acts of love occurred, I would retaliate in kind; my mom would rush into the room to see what was going on. Just as I was raising my fist to retaliate, Mom would walk into the room and catch me. "What is going on in here?" she would say, and before I could speak, Eddie Haskel, I mean Frankie, would say, "Mother,"—he always called her Mother rather than Mom, as we normally did, to get "brownie points"—"Mother, I was merely watching the *Mighty Mouse* cartoon on our lovely new 'Muntz' TV when Tommy suddenly starting attacking me for no good reason."

In my own defense, I cried out, "Mom,"—see, we always called her mom, "Mom, Frankie started it. He pushed me to the floor as I happened by." Now,

Eddie, I mean Frankie, was ever as shrewd as Eddie, maybe even more so. Having slipped by selecting the word "happened" instead of perhaps "better" or better yet "stumbled," I knew immediately I had made a grave mistake, get it "grave" mistake!

"Well…" my mother said sternly, "is anybody going to answer up or do I need to send you both to sit in the corner for ten minutes each?"

Oh, no, I thought to myself, Mom—you noticed again I said "Mom"— Mom had pulled out of her bag of punishments, the dreaded "sit in the corner" punishment to make one of us spill our guts. You see, parents from the fifties were very sadistic and kept a bag of punishments handy to keep us kids in line. Sometimes they pulled out the "clean up dog poop" one or "wash the car" and another, "hang the clothes on the clothes line for Mother" one.

However, she had pulled out the "sit in the corner" punishment. Now the "sit in the corner" punishment was only secondary to the "hang the clothes on the clothes line for Mother" one. You see, sitting in the corner is somewhat embarrassing, as none outside the home can see you. On the other hand, the "hang the clothes on the clothes line for Mother" one was devastating as the whole world could see you and even more devastating if you were "bad as dirt bad"— my term, not my mother's—when Mom would make you where her apron while performing "hang the clothes on the clothes line for Mother" assignment. I only had to do the "bad as dirt bad" assignment once, and pleaded with "Mother," applying the old the "Eddie Haskel" tactic. I said "Mother," then added another suck up term Frankie often used, and said, "may I,"—instead of can I, which Mom detested **i-m-m-e-n-s-l-y**—"may, I please, oh pretty please, pretty please with sugar on top, can I not hang the clothes until after dark, just this one time, oh please, just this one time, please!" I felt confident this tactic had worked, for I had performed my sniveling, whining and pathetic act to such a high level of perfection that I even surprised myself! Now smiling slightly to myself waiting for the old girl, probably nineteen at the time, she replied with a wide smile, "*No!* Now get your heinie out there and hang those clothes!"

Thinking quickly and in an irritating and whining voice, I asked, "May,"— "Eddie" again—"may I at least go pee first? Looking at me somewhat, but not a lot, sorrowful, she responded, "Okay."

Now I had never been considered the smartest kid in scholl, or is it spelled school, the brightest star in the sky, the crème of the crop or for that matter brightest bulb on the old Christmas tree. However, in this instance, I was, if I may say so myself, quite brilliant, did I say brilliant, yes brilliant. For I had devised a clever plan to make a sharp right into my bedroom, instead of proceeding straight, down our long, two-foot hallway. Then putting my plan into action, as I had to act fast, actually clickety-split since Mom could see down the long, two-foot hallway and into the bathroom from the living room, in which she stood. As I saw her now glancing at the *Ruff and Ready* show on TV, I quickly made my move, turned right, falling head first into my bedroom. After regaining my faculties, I started rummaging through my Halloween stuff—Halloween stuff, you say. Yes, "Halloween" stuff, as I was looking for my "Lone Ranger" mask and cowboy hat that I wore as a Halloween costume when I went trick or treating in the fall.

Side bar: Back in the fifties, all the guys would wear cowboy outfits, as cowboys were the most popular thing going at that time. Some would wear Gene Autry costumes, others Lone Ranger and still others Roy Rogers. I don't think we had any gay Caballeros living in our neighborhood, as I never saw any of the guys wearing Dale Evans or Annie Oakley outfits, for if they did, they would surely have been "beaten up." Now the poorest of the poor always wore their dad's old flannel shirt, tucked into their older brothers worn-out and oversized jeans that had been discarded a year earlier in the trash. They then rubbed a piece of coal between their hands and then rubbed it on both sides of their face to mimic an authentic "Red Skelton," "Clem Cuddle Hopper" bum look. Now for you young whipper snappers, take some time out of your busy day, from playing the latest video games or watching "U-Tube" and look up some of these characters you're not familiar with on the internet. Same goes with some of the old sayings and terminologies used in this book; it may amuse or amaze you, at least somewhat.

You see, I planned to cleverly slip on my mask and hat, once I left the house and entered our back yard. Now wearing my clever disguise, I was sure no one would recognize me. As I hung up my mother's bra, did I say bra, on the clothes line, I felt comfortable wearing my disguise. Suddenly, I heard my neighbor, Billy, yell across the fence, "Why in the world are you hanging up a ladies' bra in that silly Halloween costume in the middle of summer?" I guess by now you know the rest of the story, as I now had proven for sure that I was not the smartest kid in scholl, or is it spelled school, the brightest star in the sky, the crème of the crop or for that matter brightest bulb on the old Christmas tree.

Getting back to "Eddie," I mean Frankie. As you may recall in what now may seems like yesterday's exciting adventure of "As the Tummy Churns" or better known to you as "Tommy takes a Shellacking, While Frankie Keeps on A'walkin." As, you may remember in yesterday's episode, I stated, in my own defense, I cried out, "Mom,"—see, we always called her Mom—"Mom, Frankie started it. He pushed me to the floor as I happened by."

Now, "Eddie", I mean Frankie had now zeroed in on my "happened by" blunder, as he said to Mom, "Mother, I will tell you the Lord's honest truth." Yet another "Eddie" tactic to use the Lord's name, whenever possible in a defense case. "Mother, it was obvious that he didn't just 'happened' to walk by." Frankie then said, "Defending myself in this situation, I am an *eye* witness to the fact that the guilty party in question was actually my younger brother, Tommy, and not myself in this particular investigation." That sly old fox, Frankie was now sounding just like Perry Mason, the TV attorney, that came on TV at nine o'clock on Thursday nights. On the other hand, I was looking like the kid in the commercial that just spilled grape juice on his mother's brand spanking new, did I say "spanking" new, white blouse she just recently purchased for her favorite sister's wedding. Sinister sounding, don't you think?

Anyway Frankie, knowing that he was always my parents' favorite son, as is always the case in the first-born son, since humanity began. They also **a-l-w-a-y-s** thought he was way smarter than me, although they may have a case there, as remembering back to, "I was not the smartest kid in scholl or is it spelled school, the brightest star in the sky, the crème of the crop or for that matter brightest bulb on the old Christmas tree," may have actually proven them correct!

So, let's sum up things rather quickly! The "Chameleon" sometimes known as "Frankie, the Weasel," other times, "Eddie Haskel" and still others, "Perry Mason," had again won his case in court. As the judge, "Mom," read the verdict in open court or rather, living room, "Guilty, guilty as charged," she said. I grabbed a jurist chair on the way to the farthest corner I could possibly find. I could not help hearing my "mom" slapping "Perry," I mean "Frankie" on the back, as she exclaimed, "That a-way, Perry, I mean Frankie. That a-ways, I always knew you were smarter than Tommy. You're still my favorite son, you're still my favorite son!" After walking as s-l-o-w-l-y as possible to my lonely corner, my last thought was, at least I don't need to dry dishes tonight as Frankie would quite reluctantly do both the wash and dry chores. He! He! He! I thought to myself as I felt them pass behind my back, so "Mom" and "Frankie," who's the smartest son now!

I unconvincingly tended to act tough, but as I was a little skinny kid, I was a much better runner than a fighter! My expertise as a runner was naturally acquired from growing up as a younger brother, half the size of Uncle Frank. We had the tendency to scuffle what seemed like daily, as boys close in age tended to do. I also was an expert thrower. As Uncle Frank approached yelling at me, I would throw anything and everything I could grab to keep him at bay. Even so, I eventually paid the inevitable result. Of course, there were times of laughter as well in our home. Remembering one time, when we were little, Mom became so angry with Uncle Frank that she hit him over the head with a loaf of bread at the breakfast table. Unfortunately, the bread wrapper was torn and the bread went flying in all different directions. As all of us were picking up the bread off the floor when suddenly everyone froze and looking at each other, we gasped until we broke into a gut-wrenching laughter and Mom gave Uncle Frank a big hug!

In our small home, Uncle Frank's and my bedroom measured approximately ten feet by twelve feet and could only accommodate two single beds pushed against the wall with a two-foot aisle way between the two so you could open and close the windows; in addition a small dresser was placed against the wall at the foot of my bed to accommodate our meager clothing wardrobe. My parents' bedroom was not much larger, containing a double bed, a dresser and a chest of drawers with barely a foot or so between the bed and other furniture.

The kitchen was so small that there was no room for a conventional kitchen table. In lieu of a table, a folding kitchen counter was attached to the wall and needed to be folded upwardly from the wall and supports locked into place to prevent the counter from falling onto your legs. On the opposite wall were a sink, a small Bendix washing machine and a small refrigerator. The refrigerator had a small freezer compartment located within the core refrigerator unit that had to be manually defrosted each month. Frank and I had the displeasure of performing the task which required you to empty the contents, then place a very small pot of hot water within the freezer compartment to initiate the process. Emptying the content of the freezer compartment was not as bad as it seemed as the entire compartment was perhaps, at best, ten inches by twelve inches and could only accommodate small boxes of frozen veggies. The next step in the process was to utilize butter knives to chip away at the one-inch-thick ice completely surrounding the small unit. This typically took an hour or more and we tried to finish as quickly as possible as to prevent all the food from spoiling. Frank and I also washed the dishes following dinner, with Frank washing and me drying and placing them in a kitchen cabinet. We then wiped down the kitchen table and folded up against the kitchen wall in preparation for the next meal.

Our family of six shared a single small bathroom. It was the size of our current powder room and if you can envision adding a bathtub to the far wall of the powder room wall, you can visualize the size of our main and only bath facilities. For the most part, we managed okay, until Uncle Frank reached puberty in his early teens. As he now envisioned himself king of the bathroom, he would then lock the bathroom door and start spraying his hair with thick, gooey hairspray that stuck like glue to everything it touched. For what seemed like hours. The sound and smell of the hairspray would permeate throughout the small home as members gasped for air during the recurring ritual. Looking back, I think he envisioned himself looking like one of the "Do-Op" rock and roll singers of the era. After completing his masterpiece, he must have thought all the teenage girls would swoon over such a masterful hairdo and want to date him forever. After King Frank finally exited the small room, Dad would woefully call the local hazmat team to fumigate, otherwise it would have been uninhabitable for centuries to come! Envision, if you can, the remaining five household members lining the narrow hallway with legs crossed and tears running down their cheeks applauding the descending king.

During the winter, our oil burning heating system adequately heated our small but humble home but occasionally the pipe vent to the roof would somehow clog and smoke would fill the house. Dad would quickly turn off the thermostat and open the windows for ventilation until the oil burner technician arrived. In one event, there was so much smoke in the house the fire company arrived and several neighborhood families showed up on our tiny front lawn asking if they could help in any way as their kids excitedly ran around our yard as the fire engine sat in front of the house with lights flashing. We were immediately the hit of the neighborhood as neighborhood kids asked Uncle Frank and I how they too could clog their vent post for a repeat performance in front of their home on subsequent nights.

In the summer, our house was extremely hot and humid; so much so that during the daytime that we tried to stay outdoors as much as possible as a huge maple tree quite adequately shaded our backyard. Back in the 1950s, the only air condition to be had was located in funeral homes and movie theatres. After Uncle Rick and Aunt Phyllis were born, a third bedroom was added to the second floor which was shared by Uncle Frank and me. When it was extremely hot and humid, Uncle Frank migrated to and slept on the living room floor with the front door and back door opened for air circulation. Although cooler, it did nothing to mitigate the hot humid air so prevalent in the Baltimore area. One time during the summer, a small tan puppy meandered into the house through the opened front door, awakening Grandmom after jumping at the side of her bed and licking her hand. Frank and I of course were delighted at the prospect of keeping the puppy, but after several days, word got around the neighborhood and the owner arrived to retrieve our small and fluffy found companion. As Uncle Frank and I approached our pre-teen years, an enclosed back porch was added and we slept on the concrete floor as it was nice and cool.

During the fifties, parents did not cater to their children, as do parents do today. Parents had strict rules that were expected to be followed. Kids were told not to speak at the dinner table, unless spoken to, although that rule was not enforced, since we were too poor to own a dinner table! Additionally, kids were expected to do chores, brush their teeth without being told and not expected to use curse words, such as #!#!#! But when they did, some parents would make them hold a new bar of soap in their mouth for about ten seconds, yes, a whole ten seconds. Today, I still don't curse. See, my parents did well raising me, or was it the lasting taste of "Life Boy," get it, "Life Boy," soap in my mouth.

On weekends during warmer months, Frank and I had other jobs around the house and took turns on weekends, vacuuming the house and cutting and trimming the lawn. The second task consumed most of our Saturday, as power mowers had yet to be invented and thus, we only had a push mower. The mower contained a two-foot-long metal housing containing rotating cutting blades which were attached to wheels on either side. The hosing was attached to a long pole connected to a cross handle at the top from which to push the apparatus. The sharp blades only rotated when quickly pushed across the lawn. The mower technology was obviously not very effective as we often had to cut small portions of the lawn, let's say, two feet by three feet, three or four times while pulling the mower back and forth until it was finally cut evenly. By the end of the day, we had an exhausting workout. Additionally, weed whackers had yet been invented, requiring you to utilize hand pruning shears to trim the lawn. These two techniques were the reason it took all day to maintain the lawn. In addition, both the mower blades and shears blade required manual sharping on a bi-weekly basis thus requiring several manual hours of labor. The only good thing I got out of it was a strong grip as using the trimmers took several hours to complete the trim work and your fingers and thumb muscles hurt terribly by the end of the day.

I never realized at the time, but if my family was middle class, we were on the lowest rung of the middle-class ladder. In fact, approximately 90% of the country lived just above the poverty line following World War II as the country struggled to recover from the war years.

Life was hard growing up in the forties and fifties, as up until 1940, employers typically made their employees work twelve-hour days, six days per week. Then in 1940, the "Fair Labor Standard Act" was passed limiting the power of corporations and their ability to demand the outrageous hours employees had worked up to that time. Additionally, women did not begin working outside the home until after World War II ended. During the war years, they earned the right to work as the they were the backbone of the war effort at home. During that period, women learned the skills necessary to build tanks, airplanes rifles and anything else necessary to support the war effort. From that point forward, there was no turning back. Although everyone we knew were basically poor or some families doing slightly better, we were perfectly happy and never surmised that we could possibly be poor at the time.

Growing up in the fifties, there were no fast-food restaurants such as Mcdonalds, Gino's or Amache's as they did not arrive in Baltimore until the middle sixties. The only time I ever remember my parents taking us to a restaurant was to an Italian restaurant located on Harford Road in the city. Looking back in retrospect, it was probably to celebrate a promotion or some other special event in my parents' lives. That restaurant served food family style, as was traditionally served in the old country, as I later experienced in Naples, Italy while serving in the Navy. Whereas the owner, not a waitress, served customers the spaghetti and meatballs in a large bowl which you served onto your plate yourself. The same was true with a fine salad served in that manner and the owner continually brought out loaves of fresh from the oven, crispy Italian bread. They also provided chianti for the adults and soda for us kids until we had our fill. Back then Italian and Chinese restaurants were well known for serving large portions at extremely low prices. Even so, the meal out for our family was an extravagance as Dad most likely earned approximately fifty dollars per week, before taxes were taken out, by the local and federal governments. Even though Frank and I lived through those years, it is even now hard for me to imagine how my parents made ends meet. Unfortunately, after all these years following their deaths do I finally realize how much they sacrificed for our family. I truly would do anything to go back in time to be able to give them a hug and tell them so.

In my early years, up to about age ten, I mostly wore hand me down clothing that Uncle Frank outgrew. My family did not have very much money in those hard times. You have to remember, the average salary was $3,200 per year, the cost of a gallon of gas in the late 1950s and '60s was about 25 cents, while the cost of a new car was $2,000 and a house would cost roughly $8,500. My parents paid $7,500 for their first house and only $32,000 for their house in Fallston in 1970.

As a child, the doctor still came to our home. When Uncle Frank required child age vaccinations, I also had to get them. I remember hiding under my bed because in those days they really hurt! I think they were made from old rusty nails with a hole drilled through the middle to allow the serum to flow through and into the arm. Although there were no flu shots available back in the fifties, kids still received vaccinations for measles, chickenpox, diphtheria and other childhood diseases of the era. The most dreaded vaccine was for polio, where the doctor would have to give you about twenty needles within a one-inch diameter and it developed into a circle of puss within a few days and itched terribly. The doctor instructed you not to itch it as the puss would break which would then spread the itching sensation further down your arm.

Polio was a terrifying pandemic in the fifties. It mostly infected children and the symptoms were somewhat similar to Covid as it attacked the lungs and literally crippled thousands upon thousands of children. Tom and Tracey's Aunt Doris was one of those crippled by the disease. The most unfortunate children ended up living in a heart and lung machine for up to a month or sometimes longer, unless they died beforehand. The heart and lung machines consisted of an eight-foot tubular cylinder made from metal with a hole cut out at the top. It was a bed made out of metal surrounding the child with a hole at the top where the child's head would protrude. It was truly devastating for the child as well as the parents who would see their child lying in the chamber hoping desperately that the lung machine would save their child's life. In that respect, the disease was much more terrifying than the Covid epidemic.

Anyway, when I was young, the jeans that I wore had iron on patches in the knees to cover the holes. I did receive new Easter clothes each year unless the prior year's clothes still fit. Those new Easter clothes were very special to me as they typically were the only new clothes I received. At about age five, I did receive a new snow suit which was identical to the one worn by Ralphie's younger brother in the movie *A Christmas Story*. Speaking of Christmas, one year when Frank and I were about ages three and five respectively, we received a puppy that Christmas. We named him Skippy. Skippy lived outside in a doghouse our father had built for him as was common in the fifties and dogs were not allowed into the home unless it was bitter cold. Well, after several months and to our surprise, Skippy had puppies. That's when Frank and I found out Skippy was a girl!

My family loved Christmas, as it was and still is a magical time of the year, celebrating the birth of Christmas, Santa's arrival, and seemingly melting away the stresses of life, if only for a short time. Christmas was the only time of the year my elderly grandparents visited us in the city, as my aunt and uncle would bring them down from the country to spend the day. It also was the only day of the year that my grandparents drank alcohol as they each had a small glass of wine. As Dad was the connoisseur of Christmas tree selection, Mom was the connoisseur of fine wines, and year after year would select only the finest wine Dad could find, within our price range, for the Christmas table. For the particular year of 1958, I recall Mom asking for a vintage bottle of Manischewitz Concord Grape wine which cost about a dollar twenty-nine per gallon at that time. Back then, parents allowed their children to take a small sip to taste the delicacy. I hurriedly accepted my mother's offer and pressed my lips to her glass. As I recall, this particular fine wine was full bodied, as I believe some of the grape leaves and branches were floating around in the purple liquid. There also was an earthy aroma and minerally taste as perhaps some dirt may have been added to heighten the senses. I also noticed a hint of oak aroma, then suddenly realized there was a small piece of oak tree bark floating in her glass. Now you have to take this entire analysis with a grain of salt and understand this wine tasting adventure was from the perception of an eight-year-old boy who compared the fine wine to his favorite frozen and concentrated grape juice from the local A&P grocery store. I am sure my perception was skewed somewhat as all those in attendance at the table seemed to enjoy it immensely. Following that year's experience, I readily turned down any offers of wine tasting moving forward. In addition to my mother's excellent palate for selecting only the finest of finest wines, my father was the connoisseur of beers. In our case and being from Baltimore, his selection that year, and I believe every year following, was naturally National Bohemian Beer also known today as Natty-Boh. As dad was a heavy drinker, he would purchase an entire case of the stuff for the holidays and after visiting relatives and friends had drunk their fill, the remainder was placed on our unheated and enclosed back porch. The next summer, while playing on the porch, I spotted the beer and by final count only three bottles had been consumed over a six-month period. It truly is amazing that my father never contracted cirrhosis of the liver or ended up sleeping on a park bench in Baltimore.

Christmas was especially exciting for Dad and myself. I can distinctly remember Dad grabbing my hands and singing and dancing along to "Rockin Around the Christmas Tree" as it vibrated throughout the house from the small box radio that sat atop his dresser drawers in his bedroom, that were so prominent in those days. I was extremely excited the week prior to Christmas as Dad and I planned to acquire our annual Christmas tree from a local tree vendor lot located on Pulaski highway in Baltimore City. Dad and I awoke that morning at 5 A.M. sharp and ready for our adventure. Dad was aware of the arrival time the tractor trailer would deliver our prize, so he wanted to arrive early to snatch the freshest and best selection. Dad assigned me the task of retrieving broken tree branches lying on the ground that had broken off some of the trees as they were off loaded from the truck. Dad would use them when we arrived home to fill in bare spots in the tree by drilling holes in the trunk and inserting the branches appropriately. Dad was truly the connoisseur of the perfected Christmas of his time and I was his tree elf. Our tree was always decorated with large multi-colored light bulbs that you screwed into the many light sockets dangling from the light string. Dad always kept an extra pack of replacement bulbs in case one should, and eventually would, burn out. Next, we installed shiny aluminum star reflectors behind the bulbs that illuminated the room better. Thirdly, large multicolored glass Christmas tree balls were adorned throughout the tree. Our fourth process was to place a large star mounted atop the tree, representing and celebrating the star of Jesus that guided the three Wisemen to his birthplace in a manger. Finally, and lastly, long strands of long silver tinsel were literally tossed on the tree branches as the crowning effect. Proudly all the decorations were made in the U.S.A. as most things were in the fifties, as the U.S.A. was the China of the times following the closure of the war. The finished product resembled the Christmas tree casted in *A Christmas Story*, but ours was much grander with the light reflectors enhancing the appearance and much more tinsel that also reflected the lights throughout our living and dining rooms.

Chapter 2

On my earliest years, there was no Baltimore Beltway (I-695 or I-95). At that time, it was still farmland. When we traveled to my Grandparent Garrett's house in Manchester, Carroll County MD, it took nearly two hours as we had to travel all country roads to get there. I remember getting the willies in my stomach as Dad's car drove swiftly over sharp hills in the old roads. In case you did not know, most of the old East Coast country roads we still drive upon today were derived from original Indian trails that the Indians traveled through the woods. Those wooded trails were eventually cleared by early settlers to produce farmland. The settlers would avoid cutting down larger trees due to the labor intensity of cutting down the trees with only an axe. Therefore, our country roads but the trails, which eventually became roads still meander through the country side today due to the necessity of avoiding the larger tree stands in colonial times.

I have a family picture when I was probably three and Uncle Frank five where we are sitting on our father's vintage 1950 car hood looking down the length of our entire street which was several blocks long. As far as the eye could see there was only one other car in sight. We apparently were the only two families who could afford cars at that time. Since we lived just a few blocks from the city, most fathers walked the several blocks to the streetcar line and transferred to other street cars to reach their work locations as all the jobs of those times were predominantly located within the city. As I said before, there was nothing but farms outside where the Baltimore beltway is now located. However, by the time I was a teenager, there were, at times so many cars parked along our street, you had to ride around the block to find a parking place. When the beltway first opened and you were traveling after 10 P.M., you rarely saw another car on the road.

As teenagers Uncle Frank and I had to work after school to pay for our car insurance as our parents could not afford to pay for it as it would eat away the monies they needed to run the household. We both worked at a delivery company that delivered packages and furniture to the various Baltimore neighborhoods. During the week we worked in the return department, where we received damaged or unwanted merchandise. On the weekends we delivered furniture and on Sundays, we took a day off, as most Christians did to worship and relax. Uncle Frank also worked part-time at a Belair Road crab house where he steamed crabs in large metal vats for local customers. To our delight, the owner sometimes had crabs left over at the end of the night and would allow Uncle Frank to bring them home for us to eat.

As for being poor, or at best the lower rung of the middle-class ladder, I should have known my neighborhood was poor because almost everyone wore hand me down clothing. Another glaring sign we were poor was the habit of chewing our bubble gum for two hours and then sticking it to the underside of a table, to chew it later. There was organized baseball for kids when I was growing up. However, the kids in my neighborhood mostly played sandlot baseball on a field at the bottom of our street. We simply chose up teams from the numerous kids in the area. Since I was one of the youngest and smallest, I typically was chosen last in the pick-up games. The field we used had no infield grass, there was just dirt, thereby the term sandlot. There were no lime lines or real bases on the field. To simulate bases, we simply drew squares in the dirt. As I said, people in our neighborhood had little money to spend on extras. Most fathers were policemen, truck drivers, worked at canning factories or at better paying jobs at Bethlehem Steel Company or General Motors. In fact, one of my friend's father was a Baltimore City police officer. After he retired, he told me he had retired after more than forty years of service and had never once had to pull out his service revolver while performing his duties. Unfortunately, in today's world, I'm sure police officers cannot say the same.

Currently, the crime in U.S. cities is out of control due to extreme poverty, lack of job opportunities and the use and sale of drugs, leading to gun violence and the deaths of innocent adults and children. Within the past several months, I sent a letter to one of Pennsylvania's State Senator, Rick Perry, describing how the company I retired from had approximately ten thousand jobs in my early days working there but was rapidly reduced to less than six thousand jobs as the company and other like companies became more focused on the bottom line and stock holder interests. In the case of my company, my own observations were that the reductions were largely achieved by eliminating jobs, most of which were training or step-up positions to Journeymen positions. Since the cycle of joblessness has continued for several generations, I sent my e-mail to Pennsylvania State Senator Rick Perry suggesting Pennsylvania senators discuss the pros and cons of obtaining federal funding to reinstate training positions in most, if not all major corporations. As other, less effective federal and local programs have greatly failed our cities tremendously, I was hopeful that my suggestion be taken into serious consideration for discussion in the Pennsylvania State senate as a beginning, not a catch-all to the state and federal poverty problems. I don't pretend to be an expert in economics, political maneuvering or sociology, but none of us is smarter than the ideas and moral values from all of us. Unfortunately, and not surprisingly, I never received a response from the Senator. This is typical of both Democrats and Republican politicians who always start out saying, "This is what the American people want," but hardly ever really listen to the people or even, as in this case, respond to their constituent's concerns. As with most Americans, I am fed up with political rhetoric to improve the plight of the poor and uneducated both in the cities and rural areas of our country. How is it that we travel abroad to most other countries' cities and feel safe walking their streets and yet not feel the same walking in most major U.S. cities? As I grew up in Baltimore during the fifties and even early sixties, everyone could safely feel comfortable walking in any Baltimore neighborhood, with the exception of a few. Today, the opposite is true. You feel unsafe in the majority of Baltimore neighborhoods and only relatively safe in the best neighborhoods. This is not just a Baltimore dilemma, but a national one. If this sounds like a grass-roots effort to eliminate or hopefully reduce crime nationwide, so be it. The citizens of our country cannot depend on our government or news personnel to alleviate the crime and poverty within our country without we citizens taking the time and effort out of our busy schedules to write our congressmen, news editors and other in roles of responsibility that the apropos is no longer acceptable!

Back in the fifties, police would not allow kids to congregate and hang out on the street corners. All police officers carried night sticks back in those times. Whenever kids were asked to move on in a timely fashion, and did not do so, the officer would pull out his knight stick and swirl it around on a leather strap attached to the club, meaning he meant what he said. At that point in time the kids readily dispersed. Police were stern and meant business. Perhaps that contributed to the lower crime rate of the era. When a single murder was committed over the course of one year in Baltimore, it sent shock waves throughout the community and the local newspapers would have the murder case as a headline story for several days. How sad that in today's world, Baltimore continually has close to four hundred murders per year, and they are hardly mentioned in the news. Worse yet, society has accepted murders as everyday events that are inevitable, much the same as we would view car accidents. The statistics do not tell the entire story however, as Baltimore's population in the fifties and sixties was well over a million, and today around six hundred thousand. How sad that we have lost the moral fiber of our cities and country in just one short generation. In today's world, police are demonized by radical politicians, some news media and some well-intentioned but perhaps not well informed, radical groups. Worse yet, they are labeled as racist and enemies of black people and the poor. This is largely due to the slayings of unarmed black men from the cities and those bad apple police officers should be weeded out. How is it then that the few criminal elements within the police force are called out in public whenever a rotten cop performs his or her duties inappropriately, yet there is little to no mention of the corruption in the news media, political arena and corporations. There always have been and always will be hateful people in the world, in all walks of life. It is woefully wrong to only single out the corruption in the police force as they are our only protection between freedom in our neighborhoods and country and anarchist trying to change our way of life. Think about it, I know for sure that my generation is horrified about the direction our country has taken. I pray that other generations are horrified as well. The truth is, it does not need to be this way as our country's history proves out. Is this truly what the American people want as a nation! Think about it and let your voices be heard both as your right as a U.S. citizen and the future of your children and grandchildren's futures.

While growing up in Baltimore, I and many other Baltimoreans acquired "Baltimore" accents or dialects, if preferred, which was really slang. Growing up in the fifties, life was not as generic as it is today. For instance, Baltimoreans had their slang and, if when speaking with someone from Brooklyn, New York, you need not ask where they were from because it was quite obvious due to their distinct accent. Same was true with Boston accent, Midwestern accent and Southern accents. If visiting a city in one of those regions during the fifties, one had to pay very close attention to what a TV newscaster was saying, because of the strong regional dialect and regional jargon.

For example, we Baltimoreans would totally disintegrate words completely. "Dis" was the word this, "Dat" was the word that, and the "Utter" was the word other. A Baltimorean, having struck up a conversation with a fellow a Baltimorean, might have said to the other, "My wife said she saw a beautiful sunset last night. Did jew see it?" and the responder would have said, "No, did jew." The word jew had nothing to do whatsoever with the Jewish faith; it was simple Baltimore dialect.

Another example was when I traveled to Minneapolis on a business trip with several Baltimore coworkers. We were in Minneapolis to test out our new Siemens Energy Management System, designed to manage Baltimore's electric grid. As we were waiting for the Siemens Test System to boot-up, we were enjoying some coffee with our Minneapolis cohorts. As we sat, we shared some small talk and laughs. During the course of our conversations, one of my fellow Baltimoreans looked at me and said, "Did I mention that my wife's washing machine *went up* last night?"

"No," I replied, "I guess you'll have to forgo this weekend's poker game to cover the cost!" With that everyone laughed.

Looking puzzled, the Lead Programmer on the Minneapolis team said, "Pardon me, but what do you mean the washing machine *went up*?"

My Baltimore colleague quickly responded, "You know, it went up, you know, *went up*, it broke." Then the entire Minneapolis team broke out in a belly laugh, as one of them blurted out, "Went up, we never heard that term before. It must be one of those Balti*moran* words." With that every laughed profusely.

Then I said appropriately, "I just hope our new system does not go up while we are testing," which brought out more laughter.

A similar situation occurred while I was in the Navy. A fellow sailor nicknamed "Misery" from Missouri and I were having a discussion when he said, "Do you want to hear a funny story," to which I replied, "Sure." Misery started, while on liberty (time away from the ship), he and his wife were sitting in a restaurant, when he noticed that another fellow sailor and his wife were sitting "Kitty Wampum" from them.

"What!" I exclaimed. "What is 'Kitty Wampum'?"

"You know," he replied, "Kitty Corner!"

Now, kiddingly, I said, "I know you're from Missouri, not Mars or Venus, what, in layman's terms, are you trying to say to me?"

Looking grinningly, he said, "Kitty Wampum, you know siting diagonally from each other."

"Oh, you mean Katty Corner," I said, and we both chuckled.

Side bar: "Misery" (not his real name) begot that nickname because, well, he was plain miserable. Everything he did and felt just presented him with more misery, through his own doing! For example, Norfolk, Virginia is the largest naval base in the world and that is where Misery and I were assigned to sea duty on the *U.S.S. Guam*, a small carrier. Well Norfolk can be quite hot and humid during the summer and out right miserable in the winter, as it gets bone chilling in the winter with cold temperatures and a steady damp breeze off the surrounding waters. How appropriate that Misery was assigned sea duty in miserable Norfolk, VA. Now, not exaggerating, would wear his navy sweater, deep black, mind you, in the summer and during winter, always for get to wear his toasty warm wool peacoat.

"Dagnabbit," he would always mutter!

"What now," I would shoot back.

"Well, I should not have worn this heavy sweater today, as the temperature neared a hundred."

Or, during the winter he chattered, "I should not have forgotten my pea coat today, as the temperature dipped into single digits." I would just roll my eyes and agree profusely.

Another example is when we were walking s-l-o-w-l-y, not running, mind you, across the flight deck one day when he tripped head first onto the flight deck cracking a tooth and skinning his nose badly with blood dripping down onto his lips and deck below. How it ever happened is beyond me as the reason air craft carriers are called flat tops, is well, they are flat. The only thing I can perceive happened is that he tripped over the star-shaped "tie downs" on the deck, used to chain down the planes and copters to the deck to secure them when not in use. Another possibility is he somehow dragged his toe along the non-skid deck coating, sand paper like substance, to rough up the deck so the planes tires don't slip when it rains or snows. I also was thinking that perhaps non-skid coating was placed on the deck to give us sailors better foot traction to prevent us falling over board during inclement weather. But after serious consideration, I thought otherwise, remembering back to an episode where it proves the non-skid was not for sailor's benefit.

We were having a simulated enemy "missile hit on the flight deck drill." As I was stationed inside the "Super Structure," the rectangular metal structure that sits on the starboard, right side, for you land lubbers of the flat top. The super structure houses all the top leaders that direct flight ops and navigate the ship. They also met secretly, to determine who had stolen cakes, pies and other food from the ships "refers," navy jargon for refrigerators. Also missing were a hundred cases of marine beer rations, reserved for the marines when they play war games on some uninhabited island.

Side bar: I imagine most Americans believe that everything executed on board ship is closely monitored and controlled by officers to ensure there is no dilly-dallying going on while the ship slides stealthily through the waves of the oceans, protecting the world from the next war to end all wars. Well, the truth beknown that you could not be further from the truth. While most people visualize the professionalism of officers and sailors in the movie *Hunt for Red October*, the truth is, life on board ship is closer to the sixties TV series *McHale's Navy*. Most people visualize these sailors and marines onboard ship working extremely hard and professionally all day long, which honestly, they do. But come nightfall, the gloves come off. A movie call is had every evening featuring the newest movie releases from 1919 to 1950. As the lights go down on the hangar deck, the only illumination comes from the movie projector set high above the hangar deck. As the hangar is dimly lit, hucksters meander through the crowd selling their wares. A short, chubby guy is selling beer for five bucks per can, when a disgruntled jar-head—sailor's slang for marine—

yells out, "Five bucks for a beer that you sneaked on board ship or more likely, have stolen from the marine beer rations is disgusting, you stupid squid," sailor's slang for marines. Actually, I can't really reveal exactly what the marine said to the sailor, as my book would be rerated from "PG 2 ½" downward to six steps below "NC17." You see, marines are trained killers and they would appear soft and touchy if they could not get every conceivable explanative, they can think of into every paragraph they spout out. They increase their intimidation by snarling and salivating at the lips, and repeating Vietnam War stories. Anyway, the sailor responds, "Look, grunt, I remember you from last night, and remembered you are so tight, you squeak! So, this time I offer you the warm beer selling for a five spot instead of a cold one for six and you still gripe! If you don't want em, you don't have to buy em."

Thinking for a few seconds, the jar-head blurts out, "All right, all right. I'll take two of the warm ones, okay!"

The sailor then respond kiddingly, "Sorry, Mac, the bar's closed."

Although not to being from a Navaho or other tribe, the marine jumps up suddenly, all red-faced, and confronts the sailor, nose to nose, saying, "The bar's what?"

Quickly handing the marine two c-o-l-d beers, the sailor manages to stammer, "No extra charge for the chilies," as he knows he has over stepped his bounds with the ten-foot-two guerrilla standing before him. As he walks away, the squid's knees began to shake at the site of the marine's snarling and salivating lips.

Returning now to the missile crisis on the *Guam*, an officer takes charge of the drill, yelling loudly, and pointing at me and another sailor, "Get out on the flight deck and put out the fire created by the simulated missile attack."

As we grabbed two fire hoses, my fellow fire fighter yelled back, "Should we return to the super structure after we extinguish the simulated fire started by the simulated missile attack, sir?"

"Hell no," the officer fired back, "if you venture onto the flight deck you will be exposed to simulated radiation from the simulated fire started by the simulated missile attack."

Then the firefighter cried out, "Sir, if you do not let us back into the super structure after we have extinguished the simulated fire started by the simulated missile attack, you better have a simulated gun to perform a simulated murder, followed by a simulated court martial in a simulated Captain's Mass." Do you the reader now understand the simulated scenario of the simulated story?

Side bar: Officers seldom called sailors or grunts (marines) by name, for one good reason and one good reason only! They simply did not know their name. You see, for whatever the reason, officers are either not supposed to, or think it is beneath them, to fraternize with subordinates. It does not matter that the sailor just pulled the pilot, who are always officers, from a burning plane that could explode, any minute, from leaking JP5 (airplane fuel). Or perhaps a private takes a bullet by jumping in front of the officer to save his life.

Chapter 3

Back in the fifties, we kids typically played baseball with tar taped baseballs; that is, when the cover finally tore off the ball, we used tar tape to cover the ball. We also seldom had good baseball bats. In those days all baseball bats were made of wood, not aluminum. Just as in the major leagues today, if you hit the ball on the weak spot of the wooden bat, it would crack. Because we did not have money, we would drive a nail through the bat and wrap in tar tape so we could continue to use it. During the winter, we loved to sled ride mostly on the street and sometimes at "Jake's field," a small hilly parcel of land leftover from his farm as the majority had been sold to the developer that built our housing development. As there was little to no snow removal equipment in the fifties, we would sled ride in the streets for weeks after a major snowstorm. In 1958 we had back-to-back blizzards that laid down more than thirty inches of snow on the ground over a two-day period. We also endured snow drifts up to ten feet high resulting from high winds that continually battered the region. Our home had a covered front porch and the wind drifts were so intense that it packed huge amounts of snow against the front door and we could not open it. However, the fun part of the storm was schools were closed for two straight weeks. As I said, we had fun sledding in the streets and every so often a car would try to make it up our sledding hill and ultimately get stuck. We all would immediately pitch in and push the car from behind for it to get momentum and traction as all cars were rear wheel drive at the time. Usually, the first effort was successful, but some needed an extra push further up the hill. As always, as the car crested the hill, the car window would open and the driver would wave shouting, "Thanks, boys," which made us feel good! Whenever we sledded at Jake's field it was a special event as someone placed a metal drum at the top of the hill and we had a bonfire. This was great as our gloves would get wet and our feet cold because there was no such thing as insulated boots back then. To keep somewhat warm, we wore two pair of socks under our shoes and then added a pair of thin black boots over top to keep everything dry. Every half hour or so we would hang our non-waterproof wool gloves over the rim of the drum to dry and sit on the ground and place our feet against the drum to warm them nicely. It was really an exciting event as kids from all the surrounding neighborhoods would attend the gathering and much comradery was had by all. Not only that but most parents let their young, 8-to-12-year-old kids stay out until 10 P.M. without parent observation. On the other hand, the older kids always looked out for the younger ones and sometimes had to escort them home if there was a sledding accident or the child just became tired or frightened. Today's parents would be horrified if that happened in today's overly protective environment.

During the fifties, plastic was not yet available and containers were made from glass. There was a deposit on all soda bottles and milk jugs. Two cents deposit on soda bottles and a nickel for milk jugs. To earn money, we kids would go around the neighborhood and down by the creek where bottles would wash up to collect bottles in our wagon to cash in and go to the movies. Back then movies only cost a quarter, bag of popcorn ten cents, soda a nickel. The neat thing was on hot summer days you could stay in the air-conditioned movie theatre all day and watch the movie over and over again unless the next feature was sold out and the ushers asked you to leave. Going to the movies was always a treat, as for your quarter, you always received and viewed coming attractions, a couple cartoons and the main featured flick. Other means to earn money were cutting neighborhood lawns during the summer and clearing neighborhood snow from walkways during winter for twenty-five cents per walkway. This was a great deal for our neighbors as walkways were never cleared in a timely manner and quickly became iced over as people repeatedly traveled across them to reach work and school. Therefore, we had to carry a regular snow shovel and an extra coal shovel to break up the ice.

When I was twelve, I had a newspaper route. After school, I'd walk several blocks to pick up over a hundred newspapers that I delivered to the surrounding neighborhoods. On Sundays, I would get up at 5 A.M. to deliver more than 150 papers. The Sunday papers were approximately four inches thick because all the department stores would advertise on Sundays and there would be an entire section of funnies (comics). You can imagine how heavy those newspapers were and we carried them in a long, wide belt that went under the papers and over my shoulder. Once per month, I had to re-walk my paper route to collect money to repay the local newspaper distributor who paid for the newspapers up front acquired from the newspaper company. Our distribution center was located in the basement of a house which was located adjacent to the local grocery store which the lady also owned.

Another way we earned money was to knock on doors and ask if neighborhood mothers wanted us to purchase cigarettes or other staples from the corner drugstore for them. They would pay us a quarter for walking the three blocks to the drugstore and buying and delivering the items to their home. As I said earlier, a Coke was only a nickel, but the corner drugstore also had a small soda fountain counter. For an additional two cents, the pharmacist would add either cherry, vanilla or chocolate syrup. Additionally, candy bars were only a nickel! Another candy bar called Lunch Bar was only three cents and other assorted candies only a penny. On the opposite corner from the drug store was the confectioners store that only sold candy, ice cream and sodas, and anything sweet. Ice cream cones were a nickel and for an additional two cents you could get your ice cream rolled in chocolate jimmies (sparkles, in today's terminology). If we were energetic, we would walk the mile to Belair Road where there was a Woolworth's 5 & 10 cent store. During those days, every small and large city in America had a Woolworth's 5 & 10 cent store and as the name implies, you could purchase inexpensive goods at the store which met the needs of the country's population of mostly blue-collar clientele. Woolworth's also had a long soda fountain where there were ten to twelve seats. We thought we were big shots when we went there and bought a banana-split which consisted of a banana split in half and placed in a boat shaped glass bowel, then three scoops of ice cream were added and covered with cherry and pineapple syrup and topped with whipped cream and cherries. All that for a mere thirty-nine cents. Try to match that today when you go to Baskin and Robbins, it will break the bank!

During the summer the "Good Humor" man would ride up our street, jangling a set of bells, somehow mounted from the inside top of his front windshield. The sound "ding a-ling- a-ling" sent the neighborhood kids scurrying home to ask their mom for money to buy an ice cream bar. The kids would quickly yell out, "Wait a minute" to the passing truck and he would just as quickly pull over to the curb. Upon stopping, the driver, wearing an all-white uniform with matching white hat resembling a policeman's cap, would exit the driver's side door. As he exited one side, a kid would enter from the other side and begin ringing the bells. The driver would soon yell, "Hey, stop ringing the bells, kid," and another kid would exit quickly from the truck. The kid would then run up the street and hide. Within a minute or two, another kid would repeat the same thing and again the driver would tell him to exit the truck. This ritual typically lasted until the poor driver drove away. Although he would get no relief as the ritual would resume at his next stop. As we hastily stood in line, we carefully studied the menu pasted to the side of the truck, even though we had done the same thing twenty-eight out of the past thirty days. As I stood in line awaiting my turn, I contemplated which ice cream bar to choose. Should I select the "Good Humor bar," which contained vanilla ice cream covered with a rich dark chocolate coating, a coconut delight, containing vanilla ice cream covered with coconut, or perhaps a fudgesicle, orangesicle or popsicle. I already knew what to get as my mother had only given me a nickel which would only purchase a popsicle, as that's all she could afford. The Good Humor and coconut delight bars both cost twenty cents and the fudge and orangesicle bars were fifteen cents apiece. So, by default I always bought the popsicle which was still refreshing on hot summer days. The only kid I knew who could afford the twenty cent bars was my neighbor, I surmised because he was an only child.

Other activities I enjoyed were Boy Scouts and Indian Lore Camps. Scouting was as much fun back then as it is today. We met weekly at our nearby Lutheran Church, where my family were members. During that time, we worked on merit badges, discussed upcoming camping trips and played pool in the church's canteen located in the basement. My favorite activity was, of course, monthly camping trips in tents, rain or shine. After all, that is what us city kids enjoyed most! Indian Lore only met monthly. Activities mostly consisted of us boys dressing in Indian attire, reading about various great Indian nations and dancing around campfires, all supervised by adults. Both Scouting and Indian Lore were different from my neighborhood activities, because you got to meet new kids from outside my own neighborhood, some of which had a different outlook than my friends and myself.

Of course there were times when we had to entertain ourselves out of boredom. One such time, we were watching some carpenters finishing some stud work in a small house on a lot just north of our development. As we watched, the carpenter tossed scrap pieces of two by fours and plywood into a dumpster they had set up adjacent to the house. My friend yelled, "Hey, mister, what are you going to do with all that wood in the dumpster?"

The carpenter yelled back, "It's a dumpster, so we are going to dump it at the dump." He then said we were welcome to take as much as we wanted. Given the okay, I went home and retrieved my trusty wagon to haul the wood back to our neighborhood. Sixty days and sixty nights later, we had emptied the dumpster completely. We surmised we had enough lumber to erect an entire new neighborhood, only without windows and doors. As we sat on my family's steps contemplating what to do with the lumber, one of the guys suggested building a tree fort.

"Nah," another answered, "our parents would kill us."

Another suggested building a fort on the ground, but again the parental consent problem arose. Finally, my best friend, at least for that week, suggested building a soap box car. The term soap box came out of the thirties when at that time, bars of unwrapped soap were shipped to neighborhood grocery stores in solidly built wooden boxes that were rectangular in shape. In those days, the poor kids would snag the boxes as they were discarded, out back of the store, in the alleys. Back in the forties and fifties, everything was overbuilt, and the solid wooden boxes are an example of that. I presume the shipper was afraid it might rain during the shipping process and the bars of soap would become dampened. I assume he envisioned the soap bars slipping through the wooden slates of the boxes and onto the roadways, causing enumerable accidents. Just in case, he placed another layer of slates over the first. Good gosh, I thought, the best magician in the world could not escape one of those boxes, much less a box of soap. Anyhow, the thirties kids collected them and turned them into soap box cars, which basically entailed nailing the box to some two by fours and then adding additional two by fours as axles and finally adding baby carriage wheels to the axles. The kids would then try it out on a hill that provided a straight line of fire since the car had no steering wheel. On the other hand, our car was going to be more sophisticated as it was going to be handcrafted. First the blue prints had to be designed, which were completed in twenty seconds on the back of a candy bar wrapper, to expedite the building process. With the blue prints completed, we estimated that the assembly time would take an hour or two. Next, we each went home and borrowed tools from our fathers' work benches. The list of tools required was extensive: levels, saws, wood planes, a square, saw horses, nails and glue. After everyone returned to the assembly line with their stash, we ended up with two hammers, a saw, a ruler and a bag of various sized nails and screws.

Now for the hard part of cutting the lumber, with precision, into the exact number of pieces required for the job. To say the project did not go as planned is an understatement. The problems were many: no saw horses, no square, no glue and no levels. We decided we would make do with what we had on hand. The studs were cut by canter leveling them over the edge of a step, and the studs were scored with a pencil line held loosely against a ruler. We would then one-eye our work instead of using a level and we decided the heck with the glue, we would just use a few thousand extra nails.

Well, the few hours job extended into days, and then weeks. Cut and nail, saw and cut, the process went on and on until our carpenters work was finally finished. Now for the crowning touches: a good paint job, and some wheels. We again went to our homes to scavenge what we could. This time, we had a fine collection of goods. A quarter can of red paint, an eighth can of yellow and a whole can of blue. Additionally, we collectively obtained six wheels, one wagon wheel, two baby carriages, and two of unknown origins. After serious consideration, we opted for the two-baby carriages, one wagon wheel and one of unknown origin. We then began painting and wheel assembly, completing all in a single afternoon. When finished, what a sight to see. The front and back were painted blue, the seat yellow, and wheels without spokes, red. As we stood back to admire our work, we overlooked the nails protruding out of the wood and decided it gave our car a nice porcupine appeal. The paint job was not the greatest, even after fifty coats, and the car sat a bit lopsided as the wagon wheel and wheel of unknown origin were of different sizes. All and all it turned out grand! After waiting an hour for the paint to dry, we decided to take it for a test spin. The three of us could not even budge it, so we recruited several hundred kids from the surrounding neighborhoods to help us push it up to the top of our hill. Even with the extra help it took nearly an hour to reach the crest. We then drew straws to determine who would be first to drive, and the fattest of our crew won. As we had no bike helmets in those days, he wore a red football helmet with a white, half-inch white line hand painted down the middle. As Fatty, as we called him, sat down in the yellow seat, the crowd roared, "Go, Fatty." With that, my best friend, at least for that week, and I pushed the car down the hill. After traveling approximately five feet, the car gave out a mighty groan and then abruptly crashed to the ground. As our jaws dropped, I blinked my eyes several times, as the weight from Fatty had collapsed the car, with the wheels lying flat on the ground with the red paint facing up. My best friend, at least for that week, and I started to cry, which quickly turned to laughter. As Fatty stood up, the seat of his pants were complexly yellow from the yet to dry yellow paint, adhered to his jeans. The episode ended with Fatty stating, "My mom is going to kill me!"

Although others may view me as somewhat successful in life, I really can't shake off the poverty I endured as a child, as it's instilled in my head and lurking in my veins. Even though I can easily afford to pay full price for any reasonable item of my choosing, I still search for the best bargain or use coupons to get a better price. I also can't walk past a penny, nickel or dime lying on the ground, as doing so as a kid made the difference between leaving it on the ground or enjoying a penny candy, nickel Coke or dime bag of popcorn at the movie theatre. I tell myself it is foolish to pick it up the coin from the ground, but it's just in me and I will never be able to shake it.

Chapter 4

In the forties, there were no TVs and families would gather around the radio to listen to the news and their favorite shows. Then in the last couple years of the forties and into early fifties, TVs started to become available to the public. Growing up, we were one of the first TV owners on our entire block. The screen measured approximately twelve inches by twelve inches. Because TVs were new and the vast number of Americans had never seen a TV before, some of the neighbors would drop by and watch a show from time to time. This was even though the picture was terrible as there was what we called snow overlaying the picture which was really static which looked like black and white snowflakes all over the screen as only a small antenna that looked like and was called rabbit ears sat on top the TV for reception. Years later roof top antennas were invented which provided better but certainly not great reception. My father would climb to our rooftop to adjust the antenna to get the best reception. Uncle Frank's job was to stand on the ground and relay Dad's message, as Dad would yell down to Frank, "How is the picture now?" and Frank would repeat the message by yelling it through an open window, so I could hear it. Standing in front of the screen, I would yell back "better" or "worse" until we achieved our goal. As a kid, we really didn't care about picture quality as snow-covered clarity was better than no clarity in those early days of TV.

In contrast to today, people in the fifties were very uneducated and life was more simplistic and moved at a slower pace, as there was no such things as computers, video games, or cable TV. Most children walked to school unaccompanied by adults and arrived safely at their destination. The majority did not have great expectations to improve their lot in life as many parents growing up during the depression dropped out of school at an early age to help feed their starving, yes real Americans literally starving, families. My generation typically finished high school and only those most fortunate entered college. Our generation was the generation of cowboy movies. In the early years of television, there were only a few TV shows made for TV such as the Milton Berle or Bob Hope shows, which were slapstick comedy routines held over from Vaudeville days. During the thirties, live stage entertainers cracked corny jokes, smashed pies or squirted each other in the face to garnish a laugh. Other simplistic venues included such shows as *The Mickey Mouse Club* or *Captain Kangaroo*, where an actor dressed as a train conductor talked to a simulated farmer named Mr. Green Jeans and talked to a grandfather clock that blinked its eyes as it spoke. Another kids' favorite was *The Howdy Doody Show* narrated by a character named "Buffalo Bill." Other characters on the show included "Howdy Doody" himself, which was a talking mannequin, and Clarabell the Clown, who could not talk and drew Buffalo Bill's attention by squeaking his horn or skirting him in the face with seltzer water. This was topped off by a bandstand full of audience kids called the "Peanut Gallery" who would yell loudly whenever Clarabell the Clown tried to sneak up and skirt Buffalo Bob or Howdy Doody. Still another kids' favorite was a show called *Romper Room* where the narrator, entitled "Miss Sally," would start the show by looking through a transparent "Looking Glass" saying, "I see Tommy. I see Sue," and continued mentioning several other names before moving on to the main theme of the show which consisted of three- and four-year-olds surrounding Miss Sally as she read children's stories from a book. The "Looking Glass" was a good gimmick, as kids watching from home would watch the show to see if Miss Sally called their name.

As far as adult TV programs, they were far and few between. But one that sticks out in my mind was *The Ed Sullivan Show*. Ed provided a fifties type talent show, featuring live seals, jugglers, acrobats and other acts normally only featured in circuses that traveled across the nation during summer months. In later years he introduced to the nation the likes of Elvis Presley, The Rolling Stones, The Doors and The Beatles. Since the shows were done live and were considered wholesome, Ed would tell the performers what was acceptable and unacceptable in their acts to be performed prior to the start of the show. Elvis would swivel his hips vigorously when he sang and Ed told the cameramen to only film him from the waist up. Another example was when Ed told the rock group The Doors to wear shirts as they normally were scantily clothed during their performance. Ed would also ask the rock bands to change any lyrics he felt were offensive to his audiences. Those that did not change the lyrics were restricted from future appearances on his show.

All the earlier TV produced shows were filmed before live audiences, which was fun in itself, as the entertainers would continually make blunders along the way, which at times were much funnier than the show itself! Often the narrator found himself or herself bursting into laughter at something they had said or done unintendedly. In later years, the networks developed a method to delay live broadcasts by several minutes in case of a blunder or in case of an intentional blunder such as in the case of late-night TV, where performers would intentionally use profanity to get a laugh. As I said, these were simplistic programs, targeting a simplistic generation which made their mark.

To sell TVs to the masses and make more money for the networks, TV networks had to demise a plan to fill up additional hours of TV time with old movies. This was a massive undertaking even though all the TV networks signed off the air at midnight and did not return on the air until seven o'clock the following morning. Therefore, the networks made contract agreements with movie producers to release old movies to the TV networks to fill in the hours. To attract older and younger viewers to TV, the network executives de-cided on promoting mostly old cowboy movies from the forties to accomplish their goals. This was smart marketing as the fathers had grown up watching them in the movie theaters and the youngsters just loved anything with cow-boys in it. The most popular movie heroes of our times were Roy Rogers, Hop Along Cassidy, The Lone Ranger and Gene Autry. Later, hit shows such as *Gun Smoke*, *Paladin* and *The Red Skelton Show* were produced to attract adults more frequently to prime-time TV.

Not unlike kids of today being glued to video games, our generation was glued to the TV screen. I would guess that nobody under the age of sixty-five and still living today has a clue where the lyric, "A pair of Hop-a-long boots and a pistol that shoots is the wish of Barney and Ben" came from, in the ever popular Christmas song, "It's Beginning to Look a Lot Like Christmas." That lyric is actually derived from the popularity of kids from the fifties asking for Hop-along-Cassidy, Gene Autry or Roy Rogers apparel, cap guns and toys. Although expensive for those times, those presents pale to the cost of the Nintendo generation of today! Most people also do not understand what significance the terms "mistletoe and holly" have in another Christmas song "Mistletoe and Holly." During the fifties, mistletoe was hung from the top of indoor doorways and a person of the opposite sex could kiss another person passing under the threshold.

This custom derived from an ancient custom that originated in Norway, during ancient times. According to Norse myth, anyone passing under wild mistletoe, while walking in the woods and simultaneously passing a foe, both parties had to lay down their arms until the following day. I guess laying down their arms was a better option, in those times, than kissing your foe, as if caught doing so, you would be burned at the stake. Anyway, in modern times, this translated into kissing under the mistletoe.

As we got older, preteen and teen dances were held in our area and were called "Teen Centers" or "Sock Hops" because girls would kick of their shoes to dance. The centers were becoming very popular with all age kids and were held at various locations in nearby schools. Preteen centers featured older kids as disk jockeys, playing the hits of the day. Occasionally, a professional disk jockey would show up to spin the records and we kids thought we were hot stuff! We would then brag about it the following week in school. Preteen centers were a wonderful place for shy boys and girls to mingle. The first half hour, the boys hung out with other boys and the girls with the girls. This allowed time to do better things than mingling with girls, such as carefully selecting penny candy, such as red, green or black licorice, flavorful waxed juice bottles or splurging on a nickel Hershey bar. Then we would swoon over to the latest invention in Coke dispensers where the customer would slide his nickel into a slot located on the front of the machine and then carefully and methodically turn a crank located beneath the coin slot. With any luck, turning the crank released a super cold six-ounce Coke made with real cane sugar and not fructose as is used in today's Coke products. The difference is between night and day! After the crank released the Coke, it slid down a short shoot, where it abruptly stopped after being captured by a small closed door that you opened to retrieve it. Lastly, you placed the bottle in a bottle opener located on the machine to pry off the bottle cap, as twist off caps were far off in the future as a wonder of the seventies.

After that interesting adventure, we boys decided to mosey on over to where the girls were sitting daintily, I surmised to impress us as we awkwardly approached. As the most affluent and well versed among us would distract the young maidens with his worldly charms, another among us, who was even disgusting to us cockroaches, carefully planted juicy boogers under their chairs and then laughing hysterically, we walked away. In the meantime, and I use that term loosely in this case, the girls frantically wondered if we were laughing because their training bra or training bra straps had somehow become visible. Later, a wise guy and obviously most talented among our motley crew of fouls would cry out, "Mommy, Mommy, why can't I wear a bra like the rest of the girls," and his buddy would reply, "Shut up, George," as we all laughed hysterically, pushing and shoving one another as the girls giggled and rolled their eyes at the idiots standing before them. As that craziness ended, the disk jockey would announce a "Paul Bunion Dance" where the boys lined up on one side of the gym and girls on the other side. When the music started playing, two, perhaps three at most, brave boys would slowly meander over to the girls' side of the gym, mainly staring at the floor as they walked to hide their blushed face before selecting a girl to dance with. Perhaps five seconds had passed when the girls started walking towards the boys' side knowing that the chicken-hearted boys would never venture outwardly from their protective rooster's nest. As the girls approached the boys' line of victims, they carefully stayed clear of the dipsticks who embarrassed them earlier in the night. As the night progressed, the disk jockey would call out, "Ladies' Choice." This was an effort to get the shy and cowardly boys off their roost and occasionally convince one or two among the flock that though they were low-life cowards, there is someone for everybody. Thus is the story of preteen love as observed firsthand by one chicken among the cowardly flocks.

Years later, many new TV shows were produced especially for kids. One of the new ones was called *The Buddy Dean Show* where the host Buddy Dean would act as the disc jockey playing the rocking roll hits of the day. The show was actually produced in Baltimore and was the most popular TV show of its day as all the teenagers appearing on the show were from Baltimore, dancing to the greatest hits of the time. Everyone wanted to watch the show on TV to see if they knew any of the kids appearing on the show on a particular day. I always wondered if the kids were really from Baltimore and not from Philly, as I never did recognize anyone I knew on the show. Of course, I had never ventured further than three blocks from my home at that age, which remotely may be another reason why I never saw a familiar face! Out of that era came new dance crazies such as the "Stroll Twist" and "Bunny Hop" which later became popular at weddings. I believe it became so popular because everyone gathered around in a large circle with each person placing their hands on the person directly in front of them's hips. As music would start, the circle would slowly move forward in an awkward motion as people inched forward by hopping as they moved forward. Another plus was it required no rhythm, whatsoever, and for those a bit tipsy, a manner to remain in the upright position.

On Fridays, Buddy always had a live performer, many who came out of Philadelphia from Italian and black neighborhood as Do-Op was very popular at that time. Do-Op originated on Philly street corners, mostly in Italian neighborhoods where local kids would gather on street corners harmonizing, typically starting their songs with the lyrics, "Do-Wop, Do-Do-Do-Wop. To get the singers synchronized before proceeding into the main chorus. Although I have no concreate evidence, I had often heard that Do-Wop originated from a self-imposed slang applied to describe Italians in the forties, fifties and sixties entitled "Wop." So, to shorten the phrase into something simpler, the street singers decided on "Do-Op." Some of the vocalists Buddy had on the show were very popular with the kids such as Fabian, Bobby Rydell, The Big Bopper, Frankie Avalon, Little Richard and others. The show closely mimicked *The Dick Clark Show* which was a national syndicated program airing on Saturdays, and big named rock and roll stars would appear on that show as well.

The show originally aired segregated. Four days of the week were whites only. On Thursdays only blacks would appear on that day. Buddy would play more of the black singer hits than the white but still maintained was a mix of the two. Although that segment was only aired on Thursdays, it was still popular and very entertaining as Buddy would occasionally have black singers of the time singing live. After completing their set of songs, Buddy would interview them. He always asked interesting questions such as how the singer got started and how and when they got their big break in the business. Buddy was a pioneer of his day and pressed the network to integrate the show which eventually did happen in later years.

Although never played on Dean's show, several songwriters wrote songs with funny lyrics such as, "I won't go Hunting with you Jake, but I'll go Chasing Women." The first chorus goes as thus,

"Oh, I won't go huntin' with you, Jake
But I'll go chasin' women
So put them hounds back in the pens
And quit your silly grinin'
Well, the moon is bright, and I'm half tight
My life is just beginin'
I won't go huntin' with you, Jake
But I'll go chasin' women."

We kids just loved those types of songs and would often belt out the songs in unison. We would then burst out into laughter, as we thought they were so funny, not to mention practically all of us sang off key.

Many years later, Dad bought a "Muntz" TV set which had a larger two foot by two foot screen enclosed within a large wooden cabinet. Most people in the Baltimore area had a "Muntz" TV as it was one of the only local companies that sold TVs. Back in those days, most TVs were sold in electronic shops, however in later years, Sears and Montgomery Wards department stores sold them as well. The owner of "Muntz" TV had a TV commercial where he advertised himself as "Mad Man Muntz," meaning he was crazy for selling TVs so cheaply!

Every night his commercial came on and he would exclaim, "We got 'em tonight and tonight only, not for ninety-nine dollars, not for seventy-nine dollars, not for sixty-nine dollars, but for the low price of fifty-nine dollars." Only at age twelve did I realize that his TVs always sold for sixty-nine dollars. That amount may seem cheap in today's dollars but in the early fifties Dad probably only made sixty dollars per week, before taxes, and Mom did not yet work. Therefore, they bought the TV on layaway, which was a means to make purchases by putting five or ten dollars and then made weekly payments until the balance was paid. All appliances and major purchase were paid for in this manner, as credit cards and checking accounts were not yet available to the masses. If you needed a check, you had to go to your local bank and draw out a money order paid out to whomever you told the bank clerk to make it to.

Back in the "Muntz" TV days there was no solid-state electronics available. Those early TVs had a master controller box and several aluminumized cathrode-ray tubes that would frequently burn out and needed to be replaced or the TV simply stopped working. As the tubes aged, they would sometimes perform intermittently, and the TV would blank out. Our dad knew immediately what caused the problem and jumped into action, abruptly banging one time on the side of the cabinet inside of which the tubes resided. With that single blow, the picture would quickly return, and we would all cheer! Frank and I would try our hand at banging on the cabinet when the tube was starting to fail but after several blows, we gave up. Either Dad knew the sweet-spot or our softer blows did not provide enough force to rattle the tube. Just visualize, fathers across the greater Baltimore area banging on their TV sets and cheers going up across Baltimore and surrounding counties. What a sight to see! This ritual typically occurred night after night until finally, the tube failed all together. Then Dad would pull out the TV cabinet from the wall and take off the protective backing that prevented anyone from being electrocuted if they accidently touched the master control box which was actually a high voltage reactor, that if touched had the potential to knock you on your butt or worse. Such was safety in the fifties. It was easy to determine which tube went bad as the bad tube became totally black. Then Dad would carefully remove the bad tube and he and I would take the bad tube to the local pharmacy where they sold replacement tubes. We always took the burned-out tube to ensure we bought the correct replacement as the different coded tubes provided different functionality to the set. The pharmacy also had a tube tester to test the new tube to ensure the new tube functioned properly. If testing was successful, which was not always the case, off we went home and installed the new tube and we again would all cheer, as the picture blinked several times and finally returned.

As stated earlier, our oil burner heating system would sometimes malfunction and smoke and soot would fill the house. Applying the highly technical and mostly successful technic, Dad would apply the same style TV blow to the side of the heating system and that usually cleared a blockage in the furnace that enabled the smoke generated by the furnace to escape through the roof vent.

During the '60s, we could obtain Junior Orioles Baseball tickets for $1.75, total amount, which included seven home games in the bleacher seats, plus a free soda at each game. Back in those days, the bleacher seats had no backs and were actually made of wood. If the stadium was not crowded, the ushers would allow you to sneak into the box seats after the third inning. A bunch of the neighborhood kids would purchase the tickets and we would ride buses which, by then, had replaced streetcars to the old Memorial Stadium, located on 23rd Street in Baltimore. The stadium was approximately five miles from our home, and we usually took the bus and two transfers to the stadium and we sometimes walked home. The reason we walked home was because there were three bakeries on the walk home and we'd stop and get a nickel donut at each bakery which was the cost of the bus ride home that we saved by walking.

Today, Fourth of July is basically fireworks and low scale celebrations. But when I was a kid, the 4th was only second to Christmas as far as celebrations. We Baby Boomers all had fathers, uncles and aunts who served in World War II. Although those relatives had suffered tremendously during the war years, it gave them a deep, deep love of country and appreciation of the freedoms we have. In our neighborhood, several of the neighborhood families would gather in my neighbor's fenced-in back yard to celebrate the 4th. Firecrackers could be heard sounding off throughout the day and into the evening. Early in the morning, the fathers would drive into Baltimore and purchase two bushels of live crabs for our crab feast. This was extra special since most families could not afford to purchase crabs during other summer months without pitching in. The men would then steam the crabs on the neighbor's brick grill, and you could smell the aroma throughout our block. Meanwhile, my friend's grandmother was cooking homemade crab soup in the house kitchen. As was perfectly acceptable in those days, some of the fathers would let the kids take a taste of their Natty-Boh beer and laugh loudly as the kids scrunched up their face at the bitter taste. At night, the real excitement occurred as fathers would light-off Roman candles, ground fountains and other assorted fireworks throughout the night. All and all, it was one of the grandest times of the year for kids and parents alike. Another holiday favorite was Thanksgiving which my grandparents hosted and all my aunts, uncles and cousins on my mother's side gathered for the feast. When I was quite small, turkey was the main attraction but coming from a farming family, my uncles would grab their shotguns Thanksgiving morning and venture out into local fields kicking at local hedgerows to bag a pheasant or two. On occasion they also would bag a goose which I liked because I always liked the dark meat. In later years we only had turkey and as always was roasted to perfection!

As in most farm families in those days, the family was quite large, and we ate in three shifts. The younger children would eat first on the enclosed side porch. The men and older children would then gather around the huge banquet table containing six leaves, that practically filled the twenty-by-twenty dining room for the second shift. After the men retired to the living room to watch football or fall asleep and the kids were chased outside to play, with a sigh of relief, the women would finally sit down to a nice quiet meal.

Looking back as an adult, it was an amazing accomplishment for my grandmother and aunts to put on such a scrumptious meal in a timely fashion, as the kitchen was extremely small containing just a stove, oven combination, a small sink and a half dozen cabinets. The entire room dimension was approximately eight-by-eight and only two or three people could congregate at a time and even then, would be elbow to elbow. The refrigerator was actually located in the dining room as the house was over a hundred years old and refrigerators had not yet been invented when the house was originally built. On the other hand, Mamaw once told me that she used to cook full meals she called dinner for Pop, Uncle Toot and neighboring farmers who assisted my grandfather to bring in the crops in a timely manner to prevent the crops from rotting. Farmers in those early years did not own the sophisticated equipment used in today's world and the high volume of crops farmers now harvested in a few days took a week or more back in the forties and fifties. Because more manual labor was used at that time than in today's world, the men used up more calories, thus the need for large afternoon meals. Mamaw's dinners typically consisted of delicious delicacies such as summer soup, now referred to as chicken corn soup, fried chicken, mashed potatoes, gravy, fresh garden veggies and a cake or pie for dessert, so I assume providing those large meals over the years helped her managing our Thanksgiving dinner for our large family.

As a kid it was fun to go into the basement of my grandparents' home. Looking up you could see entire tree logs minus the bark serving as floor joists. As cinder blocks had not been invented yet, the foundation was all stone cemented together to form the walls. In one room of the basement were long, eight-foot wooden steps that were typically filled with row after row of jarred vegetables and fruit that my grandmother had put up for the coming winter months. Another room housed the coal furnace that heated the large house during the winter. If I was lucky when visiting, the coal truck would be delivering coal, replenishing the winter supply. I would snag a lump or two of coal that fell off the shoot as it slid down through the basement window and into a heap on the basement floor. To me the lumps of coal were like treasure jewels but of course, my grandparents would adamantly disagree as the coal made a mess in the side yard and coal dust went flying in the basement.

During the summer, Uncle Frank and I would spend a week at my grandparents' home and always enjoyed it tremendously as a child, not realizing why, until late in adulthood, because looking back, there was a stark contrast between Dad's family who settled in the city and Mom's farm family. Where we lived in Baltimore, the summer heat was made more unbearable by the sun reflecting heat off the sidewalks and asphalt streets, compounded by the houses being located close together. Up the country as Dad described Manchester, there was open land that allowed the summer breeze to flow more easily, and by bedtime, the breeze changed from a warm summer breeze to a nice cool breeze that let you sleep comfortably. This contrasted with our home in Baltimore where our house retained the heat from day to day unless we had a nice cooling rain that dropped the heat and humidity.

When visiting during the summer, and if we were lucky, the carnival was in town and I would join up with my cousin Janice or perhaps Jean and we would head out to the carnival together. This was a special treat for me as the summers stretched out and we kids became bored. Each year, my grandmother would give each grandchild a silver dollar to spend at the carnival and most were dated from the 1800s. Another older cousin would take us hiking in "Christmas Tree Park" which was a wooded twenty-acre park composed largely by huge white pine fir trees. It was exciting for us city kids as there was an old Boy Scout cabin and large pond located within the park, where we skimmed flat stones over the surface of the water. Sometimes, we would take Uncle Frank's BB gun and shoot at the pinecones dangling from the pine trees. This was really cool because we imagined we were pioneers hunting for food in the forest and felt really proud when we finally hit one.

Chapter 5

Refocusing on holidays, Christmas time was the most exciting time of the year and in the late fifties and early sixties, people traveled into Baltimore to shop. There were four Baltimore department stores nearly as grand as Macy's and Gimbal's in New York City. The stores would be lavishly decorated, and the store windows would display the latest in vogue toys and train sets. Each department store consisted of five or six stories, and each contained a luncheonette which was a small fancy restaurant. In the early days, Baltimore had vast neighborhoods of Germans who had settled in Baltimore and the surrounding countryside. The Germans brought the tradition of placing train sets circulating the bottom of their Christmas trees and most families, German or not, had train gardens in those days. The train gardens were sometimes lavish with large Lionel O-gauge, not the smaller HO-gauge trains of today. They always had plastic houses, churches, and other miniature buildings in the display. Miniature people made of painted steel rounded out the gardens and we would sometimes place them on the trains to have some fun. This was a special thrill for us kids, as we did not have computers and cell phones to occupy our time and it kept the kids out of their parents' hair during school break. Talking about climate change, in the late fifties, I once received a new sled for Christmas, and it turned out to be in the mid-eighties that day and a couple days following. If I had known about climate change back then, I would have asked for a bike! Dad and

I loved Christmas the most and when I was age five, we awoke at 5 A.M. to get the best shaped Christmas tree from a local Baltimore Christmas stand. As Dad wanted the perfect tree, he assigned me the task of collecting tree branches that had broken off trees when they were unloaded form the tractor trailer. We would always set up our tree the week before Christmas and Dad would use the broken branches to fill in any gaps in the tree by drilling a hole in the trunk and inserting the branches. We would the decorate the tree with large multi-colored lights that were screwed into sockets, then added shiny large Christmas balls, then added long strands of silver tinsel completed the job by topping the tree with our baby Jesus star. Think of the Christmas tree in the movie *A Christmas Story* and you get the picture. My final task was to add water to the tree each night to keep the tree from drying out. I know it seems silly now, but when you're five years old, saving the Christmas tree from dropping needles was a mighty important job. Mom really did not like to cook; however, she overcame her distain for cooking and always made sugar cookies at Christmas time. She had a cookie press gun and would insert different Christmas designs such as Christmas trees, stars etc. Frank and I had the job of adding colorful sprinkles to the top of each cookie before it would cool and harden. Mom would not allow us to eat any cookies unless the batch was a little brown. Looking back, I now know she made the last batch a little too brown, so we could get our fill before Christmas Day. Dad always sneaked a few also and we would all laugh!

Like Mark Twain's *Tom Sawyer*, I detested school. Our first elementary school was over a mile away in Fullerton and Uncle Frank and I walked to school each day. In first grade, my teacher's name was Mrs. Williams. She was about one hundred and fifty years old and, I believe, played line-backer for the Baltimore Colts on weekends. Anyway, she was tough as nails and if she caught you whispering, she literally smacked you in the back of the head with an open hand or made you stand in a four foot by four foot supply closet that had no lights for five minutes at a time with the door closed. At the time, it seemed like five hours. Also, if she caught you throwing spit balls, which were small wads of paper you put in your mouth to wet them good so you could throw them at other kids, she would smack your knuckles hard with a wooden ruler which would leave welts on your knuckles. Unfortunately, I suffered all three of these punishments from time to time even though I unsuccessfully pleaded innocent.

From what I understood from my Catholic friends, they suffered the same fate as these atrocities were also prevalent from the nuns in Catholic school as well. As for my wife Marge, she never had to endure any of the pain we boys faced because she was a goody two shoes and although trying to be discreet, would readily point out the boys throwing the spit balls. Since she attended a Catholic school on Monument Street in Baltimore, I assume she felt she was doing God's will!

In senior high school, there were basically two main groups outside a third smaller group, we called the egg-heads or in today's world the nerds. The egg-heads were easy to spot as they typically carried briefcases to carry their books and typically had their head down and their nose in a book walking down the hallways. One of the main groups was called the "hairs" or "greasers" as their attire and greased back hairstyles were left over from the fifties, think early Elvis Presley. The boy "hairs" wore their hair greased back like in the movie *Grease*, while the girl "hairs" typically wore their hair in a "beehive" hairstyle, as their hair was piled high on top of their head in a circular motion, resembling the shape of a bee hive. The second group, and the one I belonged to, was called "Joe College" as the boys combed their hair down across their forehead to mimic members of the then popular rocking roll group "The Beatles." The girls combed their hair more conservatively than the girl "hairs," so it was easy to distinguish them from the other group. The two groups got along fine, but forever what reason, the boy "hairs" seemed to get into more fights after school than their counterparts.

As I distained attending school, I sometimes hooked school with friends and we would seek out adventures to pass the time away. One day one of group said, "Let's go down to the 'Block'," which referenced Baltimore Street in downtown Baltimore within the heart of the city. Now in those days, the "Block" was famously known for strip clubs, winos and prostitutes. What better place for high schoolers to seek out adventurer! So, off we drove in our leader's beat up old Ford to seek our adventure for that day. Upon arriving, we parked along the liter filled street strewn with empty beer cans and wine bottles. In some of the doorways lay the bodies of drunken winos, sleeping off the night before's celebrations. A huckster's horse drawn wagon passed slowly down the street as he continually yelled out, "Watermelon, tomatoes, cantaloupe," as he tried to draw attention to the wares in his wagon. Wow, this place had it all!

As we slowly strolled past the strip clubs, the door hucksters would say, "Come in, boys, there's beautiful women inside to delight the eyes." They did this I supposed out of pure boredom, as they could tell we were below the legal age of eighteen needed to enter. Anyway, as we continued our walk, we happed along "The Gaiety Club" which was an old run-down night club left over from the Vaudeville days. As it was not a strip club, per say, we were old enough to enter the establishment without being carded for proof of age. As we entered the shabby interior of the establishment, it took a few minutes to adjust to the darkness as the lights were down while waiting for the show to begin. As we soon were better able to see, we took seats in the very back row as to not seem conspicuous. For whatever reason, I do not know because there were only two other people seated in the entire theater, who were old unshaven drunks seated in front the front row and located directly in the middle of the stage. I then noticed a band pit containing two instrumentalists, one playing a Zoot Flute, which was a flute containing a mouth piece located on the end, not on top, as typically seen on a normal flute. The other of the feature of the strange instrument was a knob on the side that was used to quickly change the volume as the knob slid up and down the side of the flute. The second instrumentalist played a set of drums with a large cymbal on top.

Momentarily, the lights went up and there on the stage before us were three people, a man playing a doctor, a woman playing a nurse and another woman sitting on a chair playing the role as the patient. It was obvious that the nurse was to expected show the audience as much cleavage as possible. The top of her uniform was unbuttoned, halfway down the front and a pushup bra was worn to actuate rather large boobs. As the act began, the doctor stood overtop the patient in the chair, holding a stethoscope against her abundant bosom. "Ah-ha," the doctor explained, "the problem, my dear, is that you are wearing too much clothing to let your lungs to expand properly." He continued to talk saying, "Nurse Bentley", a fictious last name, "please look at the redness in her eyes that helped derive at my diagnosis." With that, the nurse walked over shaking her behind exotically as she walked over with her back to the audience. She then bent over exposing her underwear-covered bottom to the audience. As she did so, the band chimed in as the zoot flute volume went up and down followed by the sound of the rapid of a snare drum and ending with a crashing sound of a cymbal. Next the nurse proceeded to unbutton and remove the patient's blouse expositing her tasseled breasts. Now the doctor said, "Do as I say and walk across the office floor to see if you breath more easily." With this, the patient arose and swaying her hips to and from, walked back and forth to display her worldly possessions. As I happened to glance down to the front row, one of the winos was seen gazing through a set of binoculars, to get a better view of her assets, if you know what I mean. As the show continued there were additional equally as corny and sex filled as the first. But by know, I think you get the picture. As, a teenager, I had a slight, well major tendency to exaggerate slightly. But in this case, I swear this happened exactly as I remember and telling the story to those foolhardy enough to listen. As we left the building, only the howling winos remained, taking turns with their binoculars. Exiting through the front door of the building, we were immediately blinded by the glaring sun light. As the first of us exited the building, he ran smack dab into a mailman strolling down the street. As our eyes continued to adjust, we horrifyingly realized that the mailman was one of our friend's fathers. As we hemmed and hawed, our friend's father exclaimed, "Well, boys, did you enjoy the show?" With that, he smiled broadly and continued on his route, without uttering a single word. Looking back now, I often wondered was that a smile of "wait until I get your butt home" or perhaps reminiscent of an adventure he had long forgot about. For you see, every generation has his or her memories, of although different adventures long forgotten, but still treasured.

I graduated high school in 1968 with a General rather than an Academic degree. After graduation in those days, parents expected boys to leave home and get a job or join the armed services. It was unheard of to have kids living at home into their twenties and early thirties, as is typically more common in today's world.

For most of my lower school years, I had average to low average grades as I never applied myself. Then in my senior year, realizing I had to learn to support myself after graduation, I received all A's and B's, as grading at that time was graded A highest and E failing. I won't discuss the grades prior to my senior year at this time. Reflecting back, I remember my seventh grade social studies teacher telling our class that in the near future there would be suburbs connecting Baltimore to Philadelphia and Philadelphia to New York. I thought she must be crazy, because where in the world would all those people be coming from!

After graduating high school, I signed up for a six-year hitch in the Navy Reserves, which included two years reserves, two years active duty and two more years reserves. I then went to Baltimore Community College for one semester and the following year dropped out and started a full-time job as a Junior-Draftsman making $88.80 per week at Baltimore Gas and Electric.

After two years working at the company, I was called to active duty in the Navy and served on board the *USS Guam*, a helicopter and Harrier jet carrier. Harrier jets were cool as they could take off and land vertically which was really strange to observe. Serving during the Vietnam era was stressful as people in some foreign countries would throw rotten tomatoes at us while on liberty. It was not much better at home as teenage people would sometime curse and spit at you if you were in uniform to protest the war.

Returning from sea duty and returning to Baltimore Gas and Electric, I eventually moved up to a Draftsman position and continued until the computer age kicked in and I started working in the computer field in database administration and display development via CAD technology. In those early days of computers, the data was maintained on data cards, called Hollerith cards named after the inventor of punch card technology. The technician punched holes in the database cards and then placed the cards into a data card reader to input them into the computer. This process was called a data base update. There were thousands of cards in the deck and if one card was out of order, you had to start the process all over again.

The technician then created a paper tape and drove to remote sites to load the paper tapes that used the data. A typical update took eight to ten hours. Although we more often than not worked twenty hours or more due to technical errors and card reader or paper tape malfunctions. We had to work whatever hours were necessary since the computer was down and unavailable until we completed our work. Our computer room where the computer was housed was approximately forty feet by twenty feet in size and the computation output was much less than what you have today on a typical cell phone in today's world. The computer itself was ambient temperature sensitive and if the air temperature was not maintained in the designated threshold the computer would trip off-line. Eventually, I worked my way up to a supervisory position and traveled throughout the U.S. and Canada on a team of experts with various backgrounds in operating the nations electric grid. The team would visit various utility companies and grid interconnection companies to observe how they operated their territories' grid and interconnection. We would then give presentations to their management team, making suggestions for improving their operating system and cyber security. We also documented and carried forward areas in which they excelled. Our team of experts also worked with federal agencies to develop "best work practices" for electric systems operations and cyber security for the nation's electric grid.

I also worked at BGE's nuclear power plant during refueling operations, necessary to replenish the unit's fuel rods and perform general maintenance on system components. My job responsibilities as Quality Control Inspector were to inspect any modifications to the system. Typically that meant reviewing each procedure to ensure step-by-step procedures were followed and executed properly, according to federal government regulations. This process required me to check off each step when completed by initialing each step on the document. An example would be ensuring bolts on the reactor head were properly set to the correct foot pound setting, as done with a torquing wrench. The torquing wrench contained a foot pound indicator that lit up when the required measurement was achieved.

The first time I worked at the plant, other new workers and I were required to get a full body count of the Rehems we had acquired over our lifetime for health reasons, such as x-rays. After each system outage, we were measured again to ensure we had not picked up too many Rehems. Our first venture into containment, where the reactor resides, was like venturing into a James Bond movie. We were required to wear yellow hooded coveralls in case fluids containing high Rehems splashed onto our coveralls in containment. To enter containment, we had to enter through an air lock separating the outside area from the containment area. The walls of containment are more than fifteen feet thick and of course, the air lock was proportionate in size. On each each side of the air lock contains massive steel doors, think of doors on a bank vault. To enter containment, we entered the first door which slowly closed behind us. When that door was secured, operators opened the other door leading into containment. As the door slowly opened, the air was hot and the entire room glowed "violet" from the ultraviolet rays stemming from the open containment core that permeated the air. At that moment in time, we immediately could look down into the open reactor itself, as the reactor head had already been removed for refueling. Before we could take one step, we heard a thud, as one of mt fellow employees fainted from fright of the visualization before us. The rest of us immediately stepped out of the air lock into the containment area, as the massive steel door closed behind us. The air lock procedure was quickly reversed, so the employee could be treated by medical personnel stationed on the outside of containment. And so, you have ventured into your own visualization of a new James Bond movie or so it may seem.

While performing my normal duties at the Baltimore office, I typically worked ten-hour days and attended University of Baltimore at night several days a week. While working at the nuclear plant, we typically worked twelve-hour days, six days straight with a day off to rest. We repeated that schedule weekly, until refueling was completed. The crammed work hours were necessary to shorten the outage, as much as possible, to limit down time and lesson its impact to the electric grid.

Although in today's world, you don't think of Baltimore as a Southern city, however, I remember when I was quite young, they still had minstrel shows where performers dressed in costumes and painted themselves in blackface The performers sang and danced on a stage depicting black Americans and talking in slave slang to mimic slaves. If you traveled to southern Maryland, people spoke with such a strong Southern accent, that you thought you were in Mississippi, rather than Maryland. I truly could hardly understand what they were saying because of the strong drawl.

In 1968, when I first started working at Baltimore Gas and Electric (BGE), as a teenager, I remember seeing a water fountain in the garage with a sign over top that read "For Whites Only" and there were still two washrooms, one with a sign "For Whites Only" and the other "For Negros Only." Although they were no longer used at that time, it was still unnerving to actually see them in person, especially since I had made friends with black guys, of my own age knowing they had seen them as well.

That was the same year Martin Luther Jing, Jr. was shot and we lived through the Baltimore riots. It was a scary time working in the city as blacks were protesting segregation and the way they were mistreated. When I came out of work at night, you could see smoke surrounding our building from other buildings that had been set on fire by the rioters. National Guard troops carrying rifles were stationed throughout the city and troops in Army trucks patrolled the streets as there were snipers on rooftops taking pot shots at whites driving on the streets below. There were curfews in Baltimore and surrounding counties where anybody found outside after 9 P.M. would be arrested.

When first working at BGE, I had a friend that worked in the Photography Department. He showed me photographs of black workers, working in gas main trenches with white supervisors stood over top, observing their work. There was also a picture of an old steam shovel in the background being operated by a black man.

How ironic that by the time I retired from the company, two of the black guys I worked with had become Vice Presidents of their divisions. This was a true American success story, as one of them grew up in the Baltimore projects, also known back then as the ghettos.

Another experience I had while working at BGE was I met Al Pacino, the actor while shooting the movie *And Justice for All*. He was shooting a scene at the Baltimore Corrections Facility (jail) which was located just across the street from the building I was working in. A bunch of us went outside at lunch time to watch a scene where he was walking down Madison Street carrying a briefcase as he portrayed a lawyer in the movie. We were so awestruck, we never asked him for his autograph. They filmed the scene several times and after each take, we would all cheer and he would bow and wave and talk to us. Unfortunately, most of the scene was cut from the movie.

When I was young, Baltimore had either small grocery stores or bars located practically on every street corner. The grocery store specialty items depended if the surrounding neighborhood was German, Italian, African American, Polish etc. Each neighborhood was exciting to the senses and like visiting a foreign country as our families never left our own cities and state, much less a different country. Some of the local bars had pianos where the blue-collar people would gather and old timers would have sing-a-longs, belting out songs from the World War II. Because they had little money, the local bars were affordable entertainment centers where everyone knew each other and had pleasant comradery. Back in those days, you could buy a draft beer for fifteen cents and only two Baltimore beers were served. The favorites were Gunther Beer and National Bohemian Beer, which though no longer brewed in Baltimore, is still in production today and nicknamed Natty-Boh. Philadelphia also had their local beer called Schmidt's and Pittsburgh had Iron City.

As I stated earlier, Baltimore and our world were different back in those days. Because they stayed on the same team forever, several Baltimore Colt players owned neighborhood bars and other Colt players would stop in, tell stories and hang out with the neighborhood locals. One of the players named Artie Donovan told us a story saying kiddingly how dumb the owners were for paying the players to play football because the players all grew up poor and would gladly have played for free, if provided with free beer and pizza. He also said half the team played games hung-over from the prior nights drinking and partying. Another time he told us how during a game he ran to the sideline and told the Colts Coach Weeb Ewbank he had broken his wrist during the last play. The coach asked Artie if his other wrist was okay, to which Artie replied, "Yeah, it is fine!"

Weeb Ewbank replied, "Well get the hell back on the field and finish the damn game." Artie also informed us that many of the players played offense and defense when other players were too injured to return to the game. It was especially entertaining when Artie spoke, as he grew up in the Bronx and mixing the Bronx accent coupled with the then stronger Baltimore accents was truly something to hear. Other famous, at that time, players owned some of the country's first fast food restaurants. Gino Marchetti owned one called Gino's where you could get a hamburger for fifteen cents and French fries and a Coke for a dime. Another player, Alan Ameche, owned a more upscale drive-in restaurant that served hamburgers for fifteen cents and a steak sandwich for thirty-five cents. Unfortunately, no one in my neighborhood could afford to eat the steak sandwich and we always opted for the burger. There were other drive-in restaurants splattered around the Baltimore area where the teenagers would hang out and where teenage girls wearing roller skates and long skirts with a large puppy patch sewn on the front, would bring your orders out to your caron on a tray. We also went to those drive-in restaurants to see all the souped-up cars that would hang out there. These cars were owned by somewhat wealthier kids than came from our neighborhood and some cars had had flames stenciled on their sides and loud leg-pipes protruding out the side of the car. As there was not much for teenagers to do in those days, street racing was popular, and I remember kids racing their cars on the yet to be finished sections of the new Baltimore Beltway.

Speaking of cars, most of us kids in our neighborhood had first cars that were old junkers, that could easily be fixed up by any layman of the times. Need a tune up or oil change, we did it ourselves. How about a tire change, plenty of practice there, as some of us had several baloney skins stashed inside the trunk of our cars. Who in the world stashes food in the trunk, you say? Well, it certainly wasn't us as good deli meat was hard to come by in those days! You see "baloney skins" was Baltimoran talk describing the tires on our car that had hardly had any tread remaining on them. As only mostly gas stations sold tires in those times, they threw the old worn-out tire to the side as new ones were installed. Whenever we needed "new," and I use the word 'new' loosely, we simply drove to the nearest gas station and bought four or five boloney skins for a couple bucks each. And talk about changing tires. We changed at least two tires per month, as the boloney skins didn't last long. When we changed a tire, everyone in the car would help. One opened the trunk and retrieved the jack and tire, the next removed the hub caps covering the lug nuts; they then loosened the lug nuts. This was always done while the car was still on the ground. Otherwise, when raised on the jack, the wheel would spin as one tried to loosen the snug fitting nuts. When done the process was reversed and off we went to the race. Speaking of races, we became so fast at changing tires, we imagined ourselves working at the Indianapolis Freeway.

The last thing we were good at was body work—yes kids did their own body work back then. Should a small rust spot appear, we would fill it in with body putty. A larger crack, we used screen door screens to cover the hole, then body putty in the good surrounding parts. Sometimes, we would need to replace an entire fender. Off we went to the nearest junk yard, where you could buy windshields, master cylinders, hub caps, fenders—you name it, they had it.

Unlike my grandson Caleb's favorite car, Tesla, stocked with an electric engine, all the cars from the fifties and sixties had combustion engines fueled by gasoline. The really cool cars of the era had names like the Pontiac "GTO," FORD "Mustang," Dodge "Cuda" and others. They were known as muscle cars because they had muscle powered with engines having horsepower up to four hundred horsepower. To give you an idea how powerful these engines had, if the driver floored it, pressing the gas pedal to the floor, from a dead stop, the driver would occasionally lose control of the car. This is because they were so powerful and being rear wheel drive, the car would swerve side to side in a jerking motion. To picture the movement, envision looking down at the car from a low flying airplay, the car's tires would leave long "S" patterns in the road way below. Very powerful, very powerful in deed!

Kids did not have many places to hang out in the fifties but one of our favorite hang-outs was the drive-in movie theaters. Each one specialized in different genres of the time. Bangies showed mostly horror movies, the Pulaski Hells Angels' motorcycle and action movies and still another, first run movies.

It was fun to double date with various friends on Friday or Saturday nights, as it was a full night's treat enjoyed by all. On the way to the drive in, we would stop and purchase a jug and I do mean jug or two of Mogen David Wine, the cheapest you could buy in the dollar-ninety-nine-to-two-dollar price range. This may seem like a lot of wine for a couple kids to drink in a single night but we typically had two or three carloads sitting side by side in the same row. How, do you ask, can teenagers obtain wine when under age? Well, the joint we purchased the wine from always carded us to ensure we were of legal age. For instance, one of my friends had a fake driver's license with a picture of Mickey Mouse taped over the owner's real picture. He then taped the name Mickey M. Mouse over his real name. To make matters worse, he had handwritten his name in pencil. The proprietor took the kid's card into his hand and murmured, "Uh huh, uh huh," a few dozen times and staring back at my friends face, said, "What'll you have, Mickey?" Another time and another friend had a fake driver's license with a picture of King Kong climbing up the side of the Empire State building, located in New York City. The name on the card, what else, King Cong. Again, the proprietor said, "What will you have, Ace?"

The excitement didn't stop there, as we were always breaking the, what we considered, meager rules of society. To that end, we typically smuggled in a couple or two in the trunks of our cars. Remember, this was the early sixties but most of us had cars dating back to the fifties, so the trunks were huge. We also did the same at some of the local swim clubs, scattered around the Baltimore area.

Upon entering, the gang had to find three parking places side-by-side. Once parked, each driver grabbed a heavy metal speaker which contained a wide hook on top, to drape over the top of the driver's seat window in order for the passengers to hear the movie. Sometimes one of the speakers sounded static or simply did not work at all. In which case the three cars or passenger would need to relocate.

One of our biggest concerns was that the Bengies Drive-In was located in close proximity to Middle River. Therefore, during the hot and humid summer months, mosquitos were intense. Hence you were stuck with the dilemma of deciding as to opening the windows, to have some air circulation, or closing them to keep the mosquitos out. This was a constant dilemma as there was no air conditioning in the old cars of the fifties and sixties. Also, a pain in the butt because you had to wind and unwind the windows by hand crank, as there also were no electric windows in those days. On the flip side, the winter time presented us with a whole set of different set of problems; as teenagers, as teenagers will, started necking, making out in today's terms, the windows would fog up, not that it mattered, because who was watching the movie anyway. Or for that matter even know what movie was currently showing. "Love" is it not grand. But in order to defog the windows, you either had to open the windows halfway or turn on the defrosters which were inefficient back then. Either way, it was again a pain in the butt.

After finally settling in, we typically headed over to the concession stand to pick up some goodies. Favorites were fountain Cokes, popcorn, hot dogs, burgers and for whatever reason, an all-time favorite, at all the drive-ins, egg rolls. Did he say egg rolls, you say, and I say, yes egg rolls. The only thing I can figure is that Charlie Chan, a favorite detective of movies during the forties, must have retired from show biz and opened up a chain of drive-in theatres. "Egg rolls, go figure!"

After a few hours necking and rolling the windows up and down or turning the defroster on and off to clear the windshield, it was inevitable that one of the girls within one of the three cars would need to go to the bathroom. She would then round up all the other girls in the other three cars to join them. And some holding hands and giggling would be off for three or four hours, doing whatever in the bathroom that takes three to four hours.

Side bar: How about we reverse roles. So, we go through the scenario again but this time with guys. After necking for a few hours, Bubba has to go to the bathroom. Glancing over the back seat, to determine if his timing is appropriate, he says, "Hey Mike, I gotta go to the can, you wanna tag along?" Mike says, "Yeah, let me grab my makeup kit and we can go round up the rest of the guys."

Now, on this particular night, "She'sCocked," not her real name, lagged significantly behind the other returning girls. As we waited patiently for at least fifteen minutes, we suddenly heard a scream, when my friend said, "I think that was my girlfriend's, 'She'sCocked' scream." Quickly jumping from our cars, we ran to the sound of her voice. Upon arriving at our destination, we discovered her sitting in another guy's car with him, looking somewhat bewildered, sitting beside her. Having drank a bit too much Mogen David Concord wine, "She'sCocked" had unintendedly wondered into the guy's car parked two rows over from where we were parked. To make matters worse, the other guy's girlfriend returned from her own bathroom trip saying, "Ricky,"—not his real name—"you have a lot of 'splainin to do."

A more seasonal favorite pastime was collecting and burning Christmas trees after the season ended. About a week after Christmas, as is today, people would place there discarded out to the curbside for pick-up. Only in those days there were no artificial trees, and discarded trees were plentiful. Several of my friend's fathers owned old pickup trucks. Each year as a teenager, we would hop into the pick up trucks to gather as many trees as possible into each truck.

At night all the neighborhood kids would meet down at a closed quarry, meaning it was quarried out. The old quarry, as we called it, was located along the old Philadelphia Road which in those days was considered out in the sticks. The road was actually a carryover from colonial days when it was still a muddy dirt road with wagon wheel tracks carved into the soft muddy surface from carry passengers and goods to and from between Baltimore and Philadelphia. It was the only road of the times connecting the two cities. There were and still are such named roads throughout the Baltimore area. Another such one is York Road, connecting Baltimore to York, Pennsylvania. Still another, the old Washington Pike, as suggested, connecting Baltimore and Washington, DC. And to my knowledge, the final one, the old Cumberland Road as Cumberland City or in those days, town.

Perhaps you are wondering why a major road out to Cumberland, as today it has no major significance. Well, quite the contrary, back in colonial days Cumberland was of major importance, as it was the last town west at that time. Beyond it, only wilderness, perhaps, unfriendly tribes and the unknown laid ahead. If you can only envision men, women, and children riding in a stage coach over those many miles, hardly protected from the elements. Envision still having to endure the hardships, as there were only perhaps two or three mile houses, inns with boarding rooms over top, during the course of their weeks', not hours', long journey. Image too that these often muddy and ruddy roads were sometimes blocked by fallen trees due to storms or old age. The stage coaches carried long hand saws in case of such events and all parties concerned had to do their part to clear the road. Envision again traveling on that narrow road with tree branches constantly lashing out and protruding through the windowless coach or wagon. The roads were only wide enough for the width of a coach or wagon with huge virgin trees, having never been cut, extending eighty feet into the air. The height, density and crowns of the trees had to make it appear like night time at all times, as little and at times, no sunlight could penetrate to the floor of the earth below. At times, travelers needed to make the long journey during the winter months when snow, freezing rain and wicked winds would add additional dangerous elements to their journey. Passengers also had to relieve themselves behind trees, fearful of Indian or bear attacks or something as simply being sprayed by a passing skunk. Anyone starting to appreciate modern times yet?

Anyway, the guys in the pickups would arrive first and wait for the others to arrive as they assuredly would, one-by-one. After the final car load arrived, we parked all the cars in a circle, much like a wagon train of the old west, surrounding the first load of trees located in the middle. We kept the cars approximately twenty feet away from the center, as we knew the trees gave off tremendous heat, when ignited. As the driver of the first truck ignited the first branch, with is trusty "Zippo" lighter, the flames quickly extended perhaps twenty feet into the air, as if to reach the heavens above. With that, the huge crowd, like the fire itself, roared loudly their approval. As the fire burned, you could easily feel the contrast between the hot flames in your face and cold winter wind at you back; it somehow made you feel good to be alive. As the flames roared high into the black night sky, it lit the circle brightly. People appeared in clusters, sitting on the hard, rough and, as you can imagine, cold granite floor. You could easily pick out a couple guys sitting together drinking a Natty-Boh, from those that brought along their girlfriends who snuggled together, typically with the guy's arm around his girlfriend's shoulder, as if to keep the cold wind off her narrow back. This ritual went on until all the trees had burned.

Another memory was of my father taking me down to the Baltimore Harbor as a kid to purchase fresh fish at the fish market which was furnished from fresh fish coming directly off the fishing boats. During those days, the harbor was hardly identifiable compared to the glamorous Inner Harbor you see today. There were no neat and tidy walls surrounding the harbor, as it is today but rather natural shoreline and rats scurrying around. The harbor smelled horrible as dead fish and shellfish washed ashore. There was still a large amount of swamp land surrounding the harbor with cattails growing everywhere and the water's edge had a yucky green slime floating on it. At that time, there were still local fishing boats tied to long piers jutting out into the harbor. Looking out, you could see old steam ships from the 1800s era, with rusted-out hauls that sank in place dotting the harbor and shoreline.

Remembering back to Ocean City as a young child, there was only the old town of Ocean City in those days. North of Ocean city were only sand dunes pocked with World War II era cement machine gun towers that had protected the coast in case of German invasion. I remember the first high-rise hotel built north of Ocean City named the Carrousel. It was located about three miles north of the city, really a small town, surrounded by sand dunes and was rumored to have an ice-skating rink located on the bottom floor to attract customers. We teenagers thought, who in the world would want to stay in a hotel in the middle of nowhere? In those days, hotels had no air condition, but you typically had a cool breeze coming off the ocean. Also, the hotels did not have private bathrooms and showers. Instead, there were two bath and shower rooms per each floor, one for women and one for men. If you did not spend the night at the old wooden hotels, there were public changing buildings and restrooms available to the general public. Each of the buildings also had shower facilities and small lockers to rent, to store your street clothes.

Chapter 6

Moving on to the Garretts family history, they originally came from England and in either 1600s or 1700s, migrated to Germany, and later in 1800s, some of them migrated to America. They were somewhat wealthy and one purchased or built a farm in Hanover, PA. A second was purchased or built in Sticks, PA., located just north of Lineboro, MD, just north of the Maryland state line.

The original homestead was on Garrett Road located on at the first left while crossing from Maryland into Pennsylvania on Route 30, the Old Baltimore Pike. They later owned two farms outside Millers Station which is just north of Manchester, Maryland, one of which was foreclosed upon during the Great Depression.

The Garrets living in the original homestead were very religious, and I remember seeing a family photo taken in the 1800s with a black girl in the picture. Since the Garrets; original homestead was located in Pennsylvania, I assume the girl was not a slave but a person my family took in since the "Underground Railroad" often distributed ex-slaves to farms throughout Pennsylvania and points north to families who took them in morally and also as helping work hands. This system was prevalent throughout Pennsylvania since ex-slaves had no means to support themselves once they reached the free North. This also makes sense to me because I remember my mother stating that her grandparents had taken in orphan children to live with them, and they each had chores on the farm, much the same as the biological children.

A distant Garrett relative of my great-grandfather was the first president of the B&O Railroad. He and his family lived in the Garrett Mansion on Monument Street, near the Washington Monument located in Baltimore, now occupied by the Baltimore Engineers Club. Garrett County, MD was also founded by another distant relative to my great-grandfather.

My grandmother's father was a Richarts who was English and also had wealth. He was a surveyor, and surveyed the land which was to become the original towns of Westminster and Manchester, MD. Although married to my great-grandmother, he was a womanizer. As a result of the devastation this had on my great-grandmother, my grandmother never spoke to her father again for the rest of her life once she had grown and was married. As I stated before, my grandparents were deeply religious and were from the Lutheran faith. Adultery was and is a sin and my grandmother could no longer accept her father for that reason alone.

Civil War: Our family had several Garretts who served for the North during the Civil War. Two of them died of dysentery, which was transmitted through contaminated food and water which was a common cause of death during the war. Two-thirds of the 600,000 Civil War deaths were attributed to dysentery and disease rather than in actual battles.

My grandmother and grandfather's 150-acre farm was located on Water Tank Road, between Manchester and Lineboro, MD. They had to sell the farm in the 1940s when our uncles and aunts grew up because our country was quickly becoming more industrialized, and my aunts and uncles no longer wanted to farm as it was hard and dangerous work. Because it was only with their help that the farm could survive, my grandparents were unable to continue to maintain and operate the farm.

My mother told me that the farmhouse had no electricity or plumbing as a child. At that time, the towns of Westminster, Belair and Annapolis had their own small electric companies which were later purchased and incorporated with Consolidated Gas Electric Light and Power Company which years later became Baltimore Gas and Electric Company.

Although towns and cities readily had electricity during the early 1900s, most rural areas would not get electricity until years later as it was not cost effective to extend power lines into those areas to support sporadic homes and farms. At that time, my grandparents moved into a home on Locust St., Manchester, MD. Although in town, the property had several acres and contained a chicken coop, hog pen and slaughter shed to process chickens.

When I was four or five, I stayed at my grandparents' home a week each summer. I loved visiting and always slept in the huge bed in the side bedroom. One time while staying there, my grandmother, who we called Mamaw, was making the bed one morning and for some reason I noticed that there was only one really long, continuous pillow that covered the entire head of the bed. Being curious, I asked her why the pillow was so long. Smiling slightly, she explained that when her family lived on the farm, the house was very old and had no heating system. As it was very cold at night, my mother and her other young sisters would quickly jump into this very bed, cover up with a heavy hand-made quilt and laid their heads down on the long pillow to sleep. "Wow!" I exclaimed.

Smiling even more, she said, "Yes, and since we also had no plumbing or bathrooms, everyone needed to use a bed pan to go to the bathroom, should they have awoken in the middle of the night." Grinning widely, she said, "Life was hard in those days, but we had a loving family and made it through the trials and tribulations okay." Mamaw talked that way sometimes, as she once told me she had briefly taught school in a one-room school house when she was young and before she was married to Pop. "Only one room!" I exclaimed. "Yes, only a single room," she shot back. She then explained that when she was young, there were only farms where she grew up and since the population was very sparce, the community only needed a single room building to teach the children. "Wow," I said, "that must have been a hundred million years ago!"

My grandmother would sometimes send me out to the chicken coop to collect eggs. I liked collecting the eggs, but the rooster knew I was afraid of him and would peck my legs. As a young child, I always wore shorts in the summer to stay cool. Mamaw saw the peck marks on my legs and the next day, she butchered the rooster. It was the best chicken I had ever eaten. Later, they bought another rooster to replace the mean one. He seemed to like me okay!

During the 1800s, the oldest son inherited all the property his father had owned and women, by law, were unable to own property. Pop Garrett's older brother, my mom's Uncle Oss, inherited all the farms from my great-grandparents. Uncle Oss and my grandfather were close as brothers and Uncle Oss lent Pop Garrett enough money to buy a farm and as I stated earlier was located on Water Tank Road, located between Manchester and Lineboro, MD. I remember my grandfather telling one of my relatives how the neighboring farmers would help to bring in each other's crops before they rotted. The neighbors rather than fire department came to help put out a fire in Pop's barn after lightning struck it. Unfortunately, it burned to the ground and was never rebuilt, due to the cost.

That same helping hand philosophy still holds true today. As you know, I have a bad heart and am unable to shovel snow or do other strenuous work. When it snows, various neighbors readily come over and clear my driveway and walkway to ensure an ambulance can get to me, if the need should arise. Also, people from our church have changed out all the smoke detectors in our home and had volunteers sing Christmas carols in our front yard the last two years, when we were home bound during the pandemic.

Today, you also see neighbors helping neighbors during natural disasters occurring throughout our country. Whether red, black, white or Asian, you see our fellow Americans helping each other in times of disasters or just lending a helping hand. Although those rituals seem to contradict the current political thread that widespread racism exists in our country today. That is not to say that pockets of racism still do not exist, especially in the lower class and uneducated in both white and black societies. However, I truly believe that Martin Luther's Dream, "where all the little white children and all the little black children would someday play together," has for the most part come to fruition. This I see firsthand in our own neighborhood, where children from various ethnic backgrounds play happily together. That is not to say our country does not need to keep improving race relations of all the races, so we can truly say "All People are Created Equally," after all, each of the races have contributed significantly to the success of our country. Something we strongly heard and believed in during the fifties was the saying, "Divided we stand. Divided we Fall," could not be more pertinent then in today's world, where we seem to be splintering to subsets of society that has become poison to our country and reflects negatively to other countries as they see us.

Whether through inventions, hard work or spilling our blood in wars, we are still one nation under God.

Chapter 7

Getting back to family history, the Garretts had a large family. When we were young, our grandparents had Thanksgiving and ate in three shifts: children first, men second, and women last. In total there was about twenty-five people to feed. My mother had three sisters and four brothers and we had ten cousins on the Garrett side. Some cousins, I still am in contact with.

Tragedy: Mamaw's and Pop's oldest two sons were drinking and driving and the youngest of the two was killed in a car accident. The other brother who was driving became an alcoholic, moved to Baltimore, and was never heard from again. In addition, my Uncle Rich served in the Korean War and suffered from post-traumatic stress disorder. He ultimately became an acute alcoholic and eventually became homeless, living on the streets of Westminster.

The Davidsons originally came from Scotland. Two brothers departed from Dundee Scotland in the 1800s headed for America; Tommy has my great-grandfather's Bible documenting this event.

Tragedies: My dad's mother died when he was a baby and when my dad was a teenager; one of my dad's sisters, Jean disappeared and was never seen again. My father's older sister, my Aunt Etsell, raised all her siblings in place of a mother. Later in life she married a Sicilian Italian who drove trucks and was also a bookie. He had a safe where he stashed his money which he bragged about. Unfortunately, two other Italians found out about the safe and decided to rob them. They tied up my Aunt Etsell and Uncle Sam and stole their safe. As the two hoodlums were dragging the heavy safe down the alley in back of their house, my aunt was able to free herself from the ropes, grabbed my uncle's pistol, ran out the back door, and although never having held a gun in her life, fired it into the air. The two bandits dropped the safe and ran away. It was indeed a tough Remington neighborhood and during the riots the Italian men blocked access to their neighborhood with cars and stood behind the cars carrying Tommy guns (machine guns) and shot guns for well over a week. Fortunately, no shots were fired and the neighborhood safe, during and after the riots.

On the flip side of the coin, I loved going over to that neighborhood because there was a little Italian grocery store on the corner with huge rolls of Italian cheese hanging in webbing from the ceiling and it smelled wonderful. The owner would always give us kids a taste of the different cheeses and a piece of penny candy for free! Also, although poor, the kids were really nice and we would play wall ball against a neighborhood ware house wall. Famous back in our days were pinky balls that had a lot of zip and were cheap to buy (ten cents). You could use the ball to play wall ball or curb ball which all the poor kids played in the various neighborhoods. Also, all of us boys purchased pea shooters which were similar to a straw but a little wider in circumference. You then purchased a box of dried peas to blow out through the pea shooters. We would shoot the peas at people's metal awnings and laugh when the owners would come out to investigate or shoot them at passing cars which would stop, and we would run off. At that time each neighborhood had strong ethnicity ties to the old countries, whereas there were Greek neighborhoods, Italian, German, etc. There was also an area called Pig Town where they slaughtered pigs for market, in the early days of Baltimore.

I had another aunt and uncle on my father's side of the family who could not have been more opposite than Aunt Etsell and Uncle Sam. They would do fun stuff like dress up like Hawaiian dancers and then actually sway their hips to and fro as they unsuccessfully attempted to do so in rhythm. Thank the good Lord they had seven-foot-high hedges on each side of their yard, since if the neighbors had seen them, they would surely have mistaken their pathetic dance maneuvers as severe spasms of the body, assuming they were rabid or something of the sort. Should the neighbors have seen the bizarre, did I mention bizarre, even for my family, incident, the entire family would have been hauled away and taken to the nearest nut house. As the sun gently set in the west, my parents had finally mopped up all the pee puddles around the yard from the extreme laughter we endured. Then glancing out of the corner of my eye, I spotted my aunt and uncle lying on their backs, in their now disarrayed garments, gasping for breath from their wild adventure. So ended a typical day, for a typical American family. Typical, you say. Yes, I reply. Especially since judging from the past several years, the entire country is either nuts or stuck in the *Twilight Zone*! Decide for yourself, which of the two. Perhaps, both!

Another time involves our first visit to my cousin Sammy's new home in the Catonsville area of Baltimore County. As we lived in Carroll County, at that time, we were unfamiliar with the Catonsville area. Because GPS was not yet invented, we agreed to meet my aunt and uncle at their home, also located in Catonsville. As we met at their home, they invited us in for a cool beverage and snacks before venturing out for our short, did I say short, journey. As we sat rehashing old stories, my mother half kidding, half serious asked Uncle Ray if he was sure how to get to Sammy's okay. Now if you, at all, knew my Uncle Ray, you certainly would not question as to why my mother would ask such a question to her brother-in-law. Looking a bit miffed, my uncle snapped back sarcastically, "Yes, I'm sure I can get you to Sammy's home alright. I've lived in Catonsville practically my entire life."

"Okay, okay," my mother replied, "I was just kidding!" At that point, we all could smell the slight scent of smoke, as at the same time observing an obvious cloud of smoke wafting above his head. Looking a little closer, we noticed he was now steaming from what she had said. Not being able to stand it any longer, he snapped back at her shouting, "Being a woman, you can't understand that a man can get you anywhere you want to go." Still on a roll, he stammered, "Furthermore, *all* men,"—get it, ladies, "all men" —"have a built-in instinct for directions. You could blindfold me and spin me around three times and still blindfolded, be able to point out north to you."

Side bar: Does the above conversation give you an inkling as to where this story is headed?

So, as to let things cool down a bit, I quickly suggested we all get into our cars and head over to Sammy's for an enjoyable evening, at least I hoped, I thought. So, Uncle Ray and Aunt Evy climbed into their car first to lead the procession as Uncle Ray knew precisely, did I mention precisely, how to get to Sammy's, as it was only a short fifteen-minute drive away.

Now how in the world can anybody, especially a man, with built in perception for direction, possibly get lost in a community that they have lived in practically their entire life. Hold on to your hats, you're about to find out.

Now as Uncle Ray and Aunt Evy sat patiently in their car, the rest of us piled into our cars and pulling up behind them had created a small caravan of sorts. Feeling good about himself, he surely imagined himself as an engineer guiding the train to the next train station. He gently gave his car a little gas and off we went for our short, did I mention short, ride over to cousin Sammy's. Uncle Ray drove several blocks and coming to a stop sign, put his left blinker on and waited until the entire caravan, of two cars, three counting the mighty train engine, caught up. As I said, he put on his left blinker and after we all caught up to him, he abruptly turned right, right you say, yes right. Now at this point, I thought maybe I should gently tap my horn to get him to pull over and ask about the left/right blinker routine but immediately thought better of the idea. Questing a man, especially an engineer with a built-in perception for direction, might cause a bit of friction, do you think? Well, we traveled two, maybe three blocks further until reaching the next stop sign. Same scenario as last time, stop at stop sign, wait for all the cars and turn on right blinker. And then something amazing happened; Uncle Ray actually turned right! Whew, I thought, maybe he really does know where is going after all. The next part of the trip went smoothly, or so I thought.

After approximately ten more stop signs had gone by, my wife said she thought we had passed this ugly pink house before. After another ten minutes had passed, she again said she remembered passing that house before. But I told her that pink houses with bright orange doors were certainly unusual but perhaps it's a fad in this neighborhood or something like that. About fifteen minutes later, my wife again said, "There's that house again! And there's a lady staring out the window and pointing at our car."

I blew it off and told my wife, "She's probably just pointing out the grass that obviously had been neglected for the past year." Another ten minutes passed, same pink house, as it was a delightful spring evening, our car windows were open, I could hear the pink house lady exclaim, "Abner, I'm telling you those nuts in the caravan are casing our house for a robbery," to which he shot back, "Agnes, I doubt anyone, I repeat anyone looking at this dump would want to rob it, if for no other reason then it may collapse on them as they broke in." As we slowly made yet another right turn, I heard Agnes exclaim, "Abner…I'm telling you, they are," but I could not hear the rest of her conversation, as it tailed off as we made the turn. Upon the fifth time we passed the house, I'm sure it now was the same house. The reason for my brilliant deduction was the simple observation that Agnes was now sitting on her front step wearing a very old bright orange football helmet with a shotgun lying across her lap. As she slowly rose from her steps, our caravan quickly turned, you guessed it, right, and after driving for a block and tapping my horn, the caravan pulled diligently to the curb for consultation with the engineer. After a short discussion, he somehow convinced us that he now knew what he had done wrong. He then explained that he should have made a left when he should have made a right or was it a right when he should have made a left, by now I'm sure you get the picture.

Well, we made two more rights and then a left, another right and so on, until we finally hit a straight away. After we drove a few miles, we eventually hit another stop sign. As we sat there for several minutes, a mailman stopped his white jeep adjacent to where we sat to retrieve mail from a corner mailbox. Glancing forward to the car in front of me were my aunt and uncle, obviously arguing as to which way to turn, right or left as arms flailing wildly, each pointing in different directions. Just then, the mailman climbed back into his jeep, and to our horror, my aunt, practically falling out of the car, quickly began running, excuse my French, as there is no better way to describe what we saw, my aunt running "ass and elbows" down the middle of the street, yelling, "Mr. Postman, Mr. Postman, please, please stop!" After what seemed like hours, he pulled slowly but skeptically to the curb. As he stopped, he jumped out of his jeep as if to address her assumed emergency. After conversing several minutes and him pointing left and right occasionally, my aunt returned to our car and said she had gotten the "right" directions to Sammy's house. After hours of driving, we finally drove up to the front his home, just as the local church bells rang midnight and Sammy's lights flickered and turned off. As our car windows were still open, I heard my Aunt Evy say, "Now, Raymond, what was it you said again, something about, you could blindfold me and spin me around three times and still blindfolded, I'd able to point out north to you. Yes, I'm sure you can point out north, but can you point out left?" The last I heard, Uncle Ray had bought out all the GPS devices in the greater Baltimore area. After purchasing the last one and retiring for the evening, he muttered to Aunt Evy, "I believe my internal GPS was off that night, when we went to Sammy's. I'm sure it was those 'Dang Burn' Russians messing around with our satellites again."

"Yes, dear," she replied, as she turned off the lights, to prepare for or a good night's sleep. Then glancing over and seeing Uncle Ray's face shining in the moonlight, with a slight smile on his face, she envisioned he had sugar plums and GPS's dancing in his head and had at last, settled down for a long spring's night.

Side Bar: You know you surely can't believe I'm making this stuff up. I'm telling you exactly, with a slight exaggeration here and there, this story is exactly as it happened. Now I swear, this how I remember it. It either happened that way or I'm also in La, La Land, like the rest of my clan, what is your conjecture?

Chapter 8

My Grandfather Davidson was a handsome man who lived to the ripe old age of eighty-four, which was well above average life expectancy in the sixties. This was in spite of smoking three packs of non-filtered cigarettes per day and puffing on a pipe, in between the cigarettes. As Pop Davidson never drank alcohol, it was evident that it did not lead to his death. Unfortunately, I did not inherit those strong Scottish genes, having had open heart surgery twice, once at age thirty-nine and a second surgery fifteen years following the first one. I then had a heart pump in-planted directly under my heart to assist my weakened heart caused by years of heart failure. Then in 2019, the out-flow graph became clogged by scar tissue and I was placed in an induced coma for thirty days until the doctors could determine a proper diagnosis. Thankfully, the open-heart surgery was successful. I guess I at least inherited the toughness, the Scotts are known for.

We only saw my Grandfather Davidson once, maybe twice per year. Having raised a large family, he always brought along his clippers to cut Uncle Frank's and my hair. As Frank and I were young at the time, we had the tendency to squirm when the cut hair fell on our necks. He then would flick my ear and bellow, "Sit still, boy." Sadly, but looking back now, that is the only interaction between us that I can remember.

Pop was a very religious man of the Baptist faith and taught Sunday school lessons. My father and his siblings lost their mother due to illness, at an early age. My father never knew his mother, and he and his siblings were raised by my Aunt Etsell. My dad and his older brother George grew up during the Great Depression. Because food was scarce and jobs hard to come by, they both dropped out of school at an early age to help my Grandfather Davidson do carpentry work and odd jobs, to buy food to feed the family. Dad had four sisters, four brothers plus two stepbrothers.

Dad, my grandfather and Uncle George carried sixty-pound wooden ladders plus tools on Baltimore streetcars, often having to transfer to other streetcars with all that gear to get to job sites.

Dad and all three brothers fought in World War II, Dad the Navy, Uncle George Marines, Uncle Tom and Uncle Ray Army. Uncle George and Uncle Ray were severely wounded during the war, but survived.

In the fifties, my dad worked at Bendix Radio in the sheet metal shop, now Raytheon, until he was laid-off during a recession. He later worked at and retired from the maintenance department at University of Maryland.

I have fond memories of my dad taking Frank and myself to Herring Run Park located in east Baltimore when we were young. For me it was quite an adventure. The Park was probably twenty acres or there abouts or so it seemed. It had this big old cement house that no longer had a roof, windows or floor that was fun to play in as kids. There was also a triple wide sliding board and I have never seen one like it since those days. We also visited an area graced by a large stone wall with a pipe protruding through it where ice cold spring water continuously flowed into a grated basin, for us to drink from on those hot and humid, Baltimore summer days.

In her early years, my mother stayed home as a housewife. Later, she worked part time at a local bakery on Belair Road to help make ends meet. As Rick and Phyllis grew old enough to be babysat, she eventually took a position at Martin Marietta, an aircraft manufacturer. Today that company is Lockheed Martin Marietta Inc. Later in life, she worked at Social Security and retired as a supervisor. Women did not gain legal rights to vote until 1919 and until that time, they could not legally own property. Unsurprisingly, Mom and most women of the fifties did not learn to drive until the early sixties. Mom was vey nervous about learning to drive and in those days, there was no driver's education available or even thought of at that time.

Therefore, the woeful instructions and driving lessons fell upon Dad's shoulders. I'm sure Dad dreaded the task immensely, as Mom was easily excitable! For example, when there was a clash of thunder, bolt of lightning or the sound of a passing siren, Mom let out a blood curdling scream, "**F..r..a..n..k!**" For which my father would comely reply, "Now, Violet, what can I do about it? Wait a minute, and it will go away." Now envision my mother behind the wheel of a car with my father nervously sitting beside her. To make your heart beat faster, there were no seatbelts installed in cars at that time, as they had not yet been perfected. Get the picture? Even though more than sixty years have passed since that dreadful day, the very thought truly sends shivers down my spine. If this thought does not un-nerve you, the second one will. As only more expensive cars had automatic transmissions in those days, the less expensive models had stick shift transmissions which were much more difficult to learn to drive. Guess what type of car and transmission we owned. Yep, you got it, the stick shift model. To learn to drive a stick model you had to master the skill sets necessary to engage the transmission smoothly. This required mastering four elements: the gear shifter which was located on the steering wheel column in those days; the clutch, which when properly compressed, would engage the transmission; the gas pedal; and most importantly for my father, the brake pedal. Simple enough, right? Guess again. While listing the components individually, it would seem like an easy task to learn each one in a short period of time. However, even the most coordinated individuals require a short period of time to master a co-ordinated effort to engage the transmission while slowly increasing pressure on the gas pedal to make the car go forward. Now complicating this scenario was the fact that early clutches were hard to push down all the way to the floor and releasing them too quickly would cause the car to jerk wildly, and stall. Additionally, the driver needed to slowly increase pressure on the gas pedal as he, or she, slowly let out the clutch out to engage the transmission. To complicate matters worse, the old stick shifts were not synchronized and if you didn't push the clutch in all the way, the gears would grind thusly, *grr grr*!

Now envision this '58 Chevy, bucking up and down, while **s-l-o-w-l-y** , did I mention, **s-l-o-w-l-y** inching down the street while occasionally stalling out. Now, envision standing in the street watching the rear of the car fading into the sunset when suddenly you hear, "**F..r..a..n..k!**" *Grr. Grr.* "**F..r..a..n..k!**" *Grr. Grr.* And so, this was for my mother, her first driving lesson!

Mom distained cooking meals during the week and when she did, she would typically cook instant potatoes from a box that contained dry white flakes that you added hot water to, that made a thick white mush. Needless to say, they made you gag and she would always say you could not taste the difference between the boxed and real mashed potatoes! Perhaps that was true, if you were blind and had your tongue cut out! Unfortunately, Dad, Frank and I still had all our senses and suffered tremendously whenever she cooked a meal during the week. Thanks be to God, Dad typically cooked dinner during the week when he got home from work, often spaghetti with meat sauce or boiled hot dogs with baked beans or hamburgers and veggies.

Most families had structured food nights of the week in those days. Christian families never ate meat on Fridays. Our typical Friday night meal consisted of tomato soup and grilled cheese sandwiches. Saturdays, we had Banquet frozen chicken potpies and French fries out of a box. However, on Sundays, Mom would always cook our biggest and best dinner of the week, usually a delicious pot roast or baked chicken with *real* mashed potatoes and a home-made dessert. I always asked her to leave some lumps in the mashed potatoes, so I knew they were real.

That joke always stayed between Mom and me and every year, at Thanksgiving, at her house, she would always say, "Tom, I left some lumps in the potatoes." As dinners were very structured in those days, our Sunday dinners were always, without fail, held around 2 P.M. You dare not be late or suffer the consequences!

Chapter 9

As I finished reading this book, I came to the realization that no one is truly brilliant. You may be born with an extremely high IQ or an average one. The most intellectual may or may not be successful in life, same for the average person. I have come to the conclusion that you typically become successful because your lot in life is determined by yourself, not what you're born with.

Take Thomas Edison for example. While growing up, Thomas was not considered a bright person and teachers were afraid he may never be able to be successful in life after finishing school. However, we know the rest of the story, since he went on to become one of the most brilliant inventors of our time. Did he acquire his lot in life because he was an intellectual? Absolutely not. He got where he ended up because he had a few breaks, but mostly he persevered! Thomas actually made thousands of inventions, with most of them failing. Still, he pushed on, as he believed in himself.

Now another very famous person was Albert Einstein. As we all know, Albert was the cream of the crop, right? Well you get partial credit if you answered yes. Was he born brilliant or average? Most of us would, again, say yes to brilliant. However, Mr. Einstein was actually considered mentally impaired at a young age, much the same way children with Asperger's are wrongly viewed today. We now know old Al became the most successful mathematician of our time. But are you aware that while he was a terrific mathematician, he struggled greatly in other subjects and actually failed his entrance exam into one of the finest colleges of his time? Still, he was determined to get into that fine college by brushing up on the subjects for which he was substandard. Think about it, this brilliant man's brain was unable to process the other subjects with the same ease as algebra and physics. However, like Edison, he persevered and did finally gain acceptance into the college that previously rejected him. Again, you know the rest of the story. In retrospect and adamantly having no formal training, as a doctor, I truly believe he had Asperger's as he had many of the traits associated with Asperger's. Typically a person with Asperger's traits are a superior memory, ability to understand technical information, tendency to focus on details and at times has difficulty socializing. Einstein had just about all the traits described.

Kicking this can a little further, I worked with an engineer at BGE, who I admired greatly. He started at BGE while I was a computer technician. Let's call him Mr. Engineer. Well, Mr. Engineer was obviously not the intellectual type. He was definitely a smart cookie, but was well grounded as he grew up in a rather tough neighborhood in South Baltimore. Mr. Engineer fairly quickly moved up through the ranks, holding several supervisory potions, moving up to Vice President Distribution Engineering and eventually retiring as a Senior Executive at the company. He later moved on to Chief Engineer for Maryland's Public Service Commission.

Now you may think he must be a brilliant man because he was so successful. But in my opinion, he was just an average guy that worked very hard and again persevered. Everybody liked him because although successful, could identify with the average guy. For example, when first making supervisor, he splurged and purchased a boat, perhaps the biggest mistake of his life! Anyway, one weekend, he took several of his subordinates on his new boat and they sailed merrily up and down the Chesapeake Bay dining on a few, sandwiches and having, a brewskie or two, and loving life to the fullest. Unfortunately, the merriment abruptly stopped when Mr. Captain, Engineer, accidently ran into a small object, the Chesapeake Bay Bridge. So, you ask yourself, how in the world can anyone hit a four-and-a-half-mile long bridge? Perhaps he had a few too many brewskies, you say! Maybe, he passed out at the helm of his mighty vessel or perhaps he was simply complacent. The truth is the Captain never hit the bridge, but did side swipe one of the pilings, anchoring the bridge. When asked the following Monday how did it happen, he said he honestly didn't know and asking the same question of his shipmates, they repeated the same story. The voyage may go down in history as one of the most mysterious events ever to happen on the bay.

Another time, Mr. Engineer was giving some VIPs a tour of our operating systems, on a cool spring day. One of the programs he was demonstrating was used to drop or curtail load, in case we did not have enough generation to cover the load in the Baltimore region. That type event typically happened during a prolonged heat wave along the east coast. As the VIPs gathered closely to see the process, Mr. Engineer brought up the display that initiated the program. Mr. Engineer explained, "The System Operator would simple hit this start button to begin to begin dropping load." With that, he accidently hit the start button, to the dismay of the VIPS and himself. Thankfully nothing happened because to initiate the program, we had installed a two-step process where the operator needed to select the start button and then the "execute" button secondly, to trigger the program. As I was sitting at the programmer's console at the time, I quickly said, "Nice job, Mr. Engineer, thank you for demonstrating our system's safeguards," as the VIPS laughed in relief. Simultaneously, Mr. Engineer looked over to me and gave a thumbs-up!

I am not trying to demean any of the achievements of these successful people, but merely trying to bring to your attention that the very people we look up to in life are just ordinary people like us. At birth, they were no smarter than other people. The key to their successes were identifying their strong traits and capitalizing on them.

NOTES: As a child and a grownup, I was always interested in stories and information I learned from my family members. The information,I have provided is from those memories and some from family history that has been documented.

"F..r..a..n..k!" *Grr. Grr.* "F..r..a..n..k!" *Grr. Grr!*

If you enjoyed this book, wait until my next great adventure, when I tell you how the "Davidson Clan," "Scottish," you know, was abducted by a Martian, or was it Neptune, whatever, flying saucer. Flying saucer, you say, yes flying saucer! Come to think of it, maybe that's what happened to us!

The End!

At least, I think it's the end, or better yet maybe the beginning.

Lightning Source UK Ltd.
Milton Keynes UK
UKHW022049140223
417031UK00021B/278